Distinguished Wisdom Presents...
"Living Proverbs"—Vol. 5

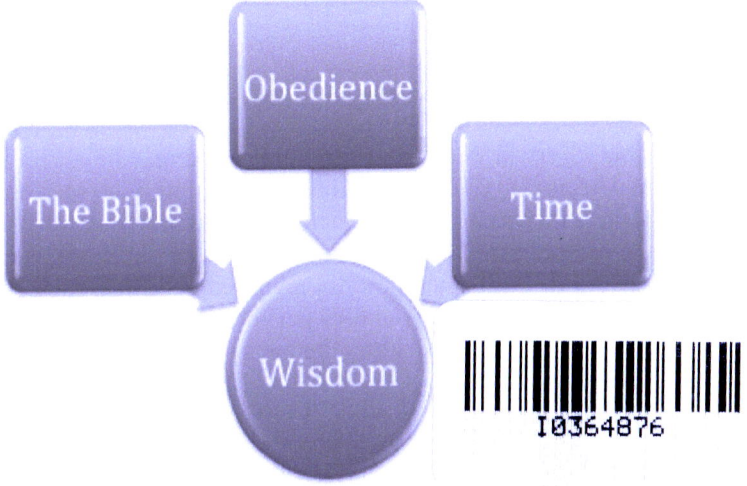

—*Over 530 New Wisdom Insights For Contemporary Times*—

Pastor Terrance Levise Turner, MBA

Well Spoken Inc. | *Nashville, TN*

© 2019 Terrance Levise Turner

All rights reserved. No part of this publication may be reproduced, scanned, transmitted or distributed in any printed or electronic or mechanical forms or methods, including photocopying, recording, or other without prior written permission of the publisher, except in the case of brief select quotations embodied in critical reviews and certain other noncommercial uses permitted by copyright law. For permission requests, write to the publisher, addressed below.

Unless otherwise indicated, all Scripture quotations are taken from the King James Version of the Bible. Unless otherwise indicated all original quotes are those of
Pastor Terrance Levise Turner.

Well Spoken Inc.
P.O. Box 291806 Nashville, TN. 37229
WellSpokenInc@bellsouth.net
www.TerranceTurnerLivingProverbs.com

Ordering Information

Quantity sales. Special discounts are available on quantity purchases by corporations, associations, and others. For details, contact the "Special Sales Department" at the address above.

Cover design by Ryan Urz/Susan of LSDdesign/99Designs.com
Book design by Terrance L. Turner

Printed in the United States of America

ISBN	9781733979634	and	9781733979658	paperback
ISBN	9781733979665	and	9781733979641	hardcover

Also by Pastor Terrance Levise Turner, MBA:

Distinguished Wisdom Presents... Living Proverbs–Volume 1

Distinguished Wisdom Presents... Living Proverbs–Volume 2

Distinguished Wisdom Presents... Living Proverbs–Volume 3

Distinguished Wisdom Presents... Living Proverbs–Volume 4

Distinguished Wisdom Presents... The Dynamic Victory Confession: Powerful Confessions For A Victorious Life!

The Earth Is Sad, Little Timmy

Distinguished Wisdom Presents... Your Wealth Is In Your Anointing: Discover Keys To Releasing Your Potential.

This book is dedicated to young people of today and in future generations. I desire that they have a solid understanding of God and His principles for life; and thereby have a successful, prosperous, safe, and godly life.

Contents

Acknowledgments	VII
Preface	IX
Introduction	XI
"Living Proverbs" –Vol. 5	1
Final Word	273
About The Author	276

Acknowledgments

I would like to acknowledge the love and support of my wife, Dr. Avis Turner. She is my partner in life, and the gift that God has given me to help accomplish His purposes in life. Her support and encouragement has helped to enable me to reach the potential God has invested in me. She is a *true* wife. We are better together, and together God is enabling us to reach the world.

Again, I would like to give everlasting thanks to my mother, Geraldine Key, for the foundation of truth and example she laid for my brothers and I. She is the reason I know God as my Heavenly Father and the Lord Jesus Christ as my Savior. She continues to be a support and encouragement as I strive to fulfill God's purposes for my life.

I acknowledge the solid example of faith, faithfulness, and morality that I gained from my grandmother, Wilma Starks, and grandfather, Clarence Young. They both were sources of stability in my life. Their examples will continue to live on in all that I do.

I thank God for all the teachers and preachers of wisdom and instruction over my lifetime. Thank God for Rev. Brockway, Bishop Phillip Gardner, missionary Mary Archie, Pastor Charles Cowan, Bishop T.D. Jakes, Joyce Meyer, Dr. Mike Murdock, and many others that has inspired my life. Thank God for inspirational and motivational teachers, such as Les Brown, Brian Tracy, Dr. John Maxwell; as well as great leaders in our society, such as Gen. Colin Powell. Also, I recognize the impact of great educational leaders upon my life, such as the late Dr. James A. Hefner, former president of Tennessee State University. My life has been impacted by great leaders in wisdom, instruction, and by example. My mother laid the foundation, and Jehovah God my Heavenly Father has built upon that foundation the right keystones, starting with my wife, Dr. Avis Turner, for a successful life.

Preface

My mother introduced my brothers and I, to God as our Father by teaching us the principles of the Book of Proverbs in the Bible. She sat down with us in Bible studies and prayer, and taught us the principles of morality, godliness, and wisdom for life that the Book of Proverbs contained. She took us to church and she lived the principles of God's Word before us in our home. My mother's dedication to the Lord Jesus Christ was my example for seeing how to live a life sanctified unto God. Through her example, along with my grandmother, I gained a deep love for God and His principles.

As I grew up and became an adult, I continued to look to God's Word as the source of wisdom for life. The Book of Proverbs became a mainstay of reliable wisdom for my life. The structure of the book and the manner in which the truths were conveyed were easy for me to digest. They are direct, bite-sized, concentrated nuggets of truth. This affected and helped to craft and shape my thinking.

Distinguished Wisdom Presents... Living Proverbs came into being gradually, day by day. I was led by God to begin sharing the wisdom, which I had learned and ascertained from walking with Him, with others that could be enlighten and encouraged by what was offered.

Living Proverbs came into being in real-time being led by the Spirit and sharing with others what I believed would minister to their lives. My prayer is that they will minister to you now and in time to come.

Pastor Terrance Levise Turner, MBA

Introduction

Historical Aspects of Biblical Proverbs

1 Kings 3:4–14 gives the account of King Solomon becoming king after his father King David died. He, though a full grown man, felt as if he was a child in regards to taking over such an immense responsibility to reign as king, especially after such a notable mark, which his father had made on the kingdom of Israel and history.

Solomon prayed to God for wisdom to rule justly and with good understanding for Gods people. The following passage describes the account:

> And the king went to Gibeon to sacrifice there; for that was the great high place: a thousand burnt offerings did Solomon offer upon that altar.
>
> In Gibeon the Lord appeared to Solomon in a dream by night: and God said, Ask what I shall give thee.
>
> And Solomon said, Thou hast shewed unto thy servant David my father great mercy, according

as he walked before thee in truth, and in righteousness, and in uprightness of heart with thee; and thou hast kept for him this great kindness, that thou hast given him a son to sit on his throne, as it is this day.

And now, O Lord my God, thou hast made thy servant king instead of David my father: and I am but a little child: I know not how to go out or come in.

And thy servant is in the midst of thy people which thou hast chosen, a great people, that cannot be numbered nor counted for multitude.

Give therefore thy servant an understanding heart to judge thy people, that I may discern between good and bad: for who is able to judge this thy so great a people?

And the speech pleased the Lord, that Solomon had asked this thing.

And God said unto him, Because thou hast asked this thing, and hast not asked for thyself long life; neither hast asked riches for thyself, nor hast asked the life of thine enemies; but hast asked for thyself understanding to discern judgment;

Behold, I have done according to thy words: lo, I have given thee a wise and an understanding heart; so that there was none like thee before thee, neither after thee shall any arise like unto thee.

And I have also given thee that which thou hast not asked, both riches, and honour: so that there shall not be any among the kings like unto thee all thy days.

And if thou wilt walk in my ways, to keep my statutes and my commandments, as thy father David did walk, then I will lengthen thy days.

–1 Kings 3:4–14

So, we see that God gave King Solomon wisdom to reign over His people; unlike any other king. The wisdom, which Solomon obtained, was the key to great riches, honor, and renown.

Solomon was a teacher. He was a preacher as well. He taught his sons and others his wisdom using proverbs, parables, and wise sayings. He felt that this was the best way to help those that heard his wisdom to gain the concepts, which he was attempting to convey to their understanding.

In Ecclesiastes 1:1 King Solomon calls himself the Preacher. This is what it says:

> The words of the Preacher, the son of David, king in Jerusalem.
>
> –Ecclesiastes 1:1

The Book of Proverbs also gives us the biblical purpose of using proverbs, parables, and wise sayings to teach. Proverbs 1:1–7 defines the purpose of the Book of Proverbs, as well as the purpose of this book **Living Proverbs**. This is what it says:

> The proverbs of Solomon the son of David, king of Israel;
>
> To **know** wisdom and instruction; to **perceive** the words of understanding;
>
> To **receive** the instruction of wisdom, justice, and judgment, and equity;
>
> To give **subtilty** to the simple, to the young man knowledge and discretion.
>
> A wise man will hear, and will increase learning; and a man of understanding shall attain unto wise counsels:
>
> To **understand** a proverb, and the **interpretation**; the words of the wise, and their dark sayings.
>
> The fear of the Lord is the beginning of knowledge: but fools despise wisdom and instruction.

Pastor Terrance Levise Turner, MBA

—Proverbs 1:1–7

Notice, that I bolded a few key words in this passage of scripture, which I would like to point out to you; they clearly explain the purpose of the biblical Book of Proverbs, as well as this book **Living Proverbs**.

The first word that I would like to point out is the word **"know."**

The Strong's Exhaustive Concordance of The Bible defines this word like this:

> **3045– yada**
>
> 1. to know or ascertain by seeing
>
> 2. observation, recognition, instruction
>
> 3. acknowledge, acquainted with
>
> 4. to know assuredly
>
> 5. to be aware
>
> 6. to know for a certainty
>
> 7. to cause to discern
>
> 8. to discover

Therefore, based on these definitions, we see that the initial purpose of biblical proverbs is so that the reader may know and ascertain Gods wisdom by clearly seeing it. It is to allow the person to observe the deeper meaning of a subject in a condensed way. It is to teach the person how to recognize wisdom when it is being spoken, and to take heed to instruction when it is being given.

The speaking of proverbs is a way of conveying meaning that has been tested and tried as true; and it is a way of conveying those truths to others in a condensed manner that they can gain the certainty of those truths.

They are given so that people can discern truth when it is being presented, without having to have a full explanation. They will not have to have a full explanation in order to discern the meaning that is being conveyed.

Proverbs are a condensed conveying of deeper meaning.

The next word, which King Solomon uses to define the purpose of biblical proverbs is **perceive**. This is how the concordance defines it:

> 995–**biyn**
>
> 1. To separate mentally or to distinguish
>
> 2. understand
>
> 3. discern
>
> 4. be cunning

Pastor Terrance Levise Turner, MBA

    5. diligently

    6. direct

    7. to have intelligence

    8. deal wisely

Notice, the words used to define perceive are words that deal with the mind. One of the purposes of proverbs of all kinds is for the reader to become more keen in their thinking, and thus, more capable to be successful in life.

The goal is that the person that heeds proverbs will learn to perceive and understand Gods ways of doing and being right in life. It is that they will learn to discern right and wrong, as well as timing and manner of doing the right thing.

Through studying proverbs a young person, as well as those more experienced in life, will become more cunning or skillful in navigating decisions, people skills, etc. Various proverbs are given to encourage the reader to become more diligent in life matters; and thus more successful and prosperous.

Short wise sayings, parables, and proverbs can provide swift guidance to a person's decision making. They will direct a persons steps in the midst of a decision making process.

Through heeding various godly proverbs, a person will gain quick intelligence for good judgment. The person that gives themselves to proverbs as a companion to their life will learn to deal wisely in life's diverse situations.

As a person gives themselves to the study of proverbs, they will learn to **receive** wisdom when it is being presented. They will gain more **subtlety** in life. They will become more discreet and refined in behavior and decision-making and manner; thus, making them better able to smoothly navigate the potentially rough matters of human relationships.

Ultimately, the biblical Book of Proverbs, as well as this book **Living Proverbs** is written so that the person that heeds them may gain a greater **understanding** of Gods principles for successful living; and that they will be able to **interpret** Gods wisdom as it is presented to them; whether through reading the Bible or in the lessons of life.

This is the purpose of this book **Living Proverbs.** My goal in writing this book is to convey the understanding of the Word of God and Gods principles in such a way that it is easy for anyone to understand. My goal is to bring Gods Word alive to your understanding.

Insights On Wisdom

What is wisdom? Why is it important? How is it obtained? How is it used?

Wisdom is not knowledge. Wisdom is the discerned, proper application of knowledge, which comes from experience. In this book I utilize several key conceptual scriptural more than once. However, with each usage I bring out a unique perspective or point. The wisdom of God's Word is multifaceted. There are layers of truth to be discovered. The name of the book series is ***Distinguished Wisdom Presents . . .***

"Living Proverbs." Each *wisdom nugget* reveals a treasure of truth that has been extracted and refined by understanding. The deeper meaning is conveyed by a few unique and memorable words. The Book of Proverbs in the Bible encourages us to not only get knowledge of the wisdom of God, but to get "understanding".

> Get wisdom, get understanding: forget it not; neither decline from the words of my mouth. Forsake her not, and she shall preserve thee: love her, and she shall keep thee. Wisdom is the principle thing; therefore, get wisdom; and with all thy getting get understanding.
>
> – Proverbs 4: 5–7

Romans 10:17 says, "Faith comes by hearing, and hearing by the Word of God." As you continue to abide in the principles of God's Word, you gain deeper understanding. The Word becomes more usable to you. God wants us to be skillful in the use of His Word for our daily living.

The following scriptures further emphasize the vital importance of wisdom:

> The fear of the Lord is the beginning of knowledge: but fools despise wisdom and instruction.
>
> – Proverbs 1:7

Also, that the soul be without knowledge, it is not good; and he that hasteth with the feet sinneth.

– Proverbs 19:2

He that getteth wisdom loveth his own soul: he that keepeth understanding shall find good.

– Proverbs 19:8

Based on these scriptures, we can see that Gods wisdom is vital for successful living. **Distinguished Wisdom Presents... Living Proverbs –Vol. 5**, helps to further your understanding and application of God's wisdom for life.

Habakkuk 2:4b says, " . . . *the just shall live by his faith.*" In other words, the only way that the faith and wisdom of the Word of God will work for you is by actually living by what we learn. As God's Word is lived out in our daily life, it becomes wisdom gained by experience. We are then able to know with certainty, the reliability of Gods Word. We can then pass that wisdom on to our family, friends, and those we come in contact with in our daily life.

Wisdom is for success in daily living. These **Living Proverbs** came in response addressing to the challenges of my life and the lives of others. They are original, relevant, Christian wisdom quotes that will help you on your journey. I have dealt with many of the same challenges that you have, and I know God's Word will work for you.

The Purpose of *Living Proverbs*.

The purpose of *Living Proverbs* is derived from the purpose of my company Well Spoken Incorporated in Nashville, Tennessee. In 2005, God inspired me to start a company with the purpose of communicating the spoken word in a clear, distinct manner that easily conveyed understanding to the listener. Our primary product at the start was audio books. We have since expanded into print, speaking, and other forms of media.

The foundational scripture that inspired the company is Nehemiah 8:7–8. It says,

> Also Jeshua, and Bani, and Sherebiah, Jamin, Akkub, Shabbethai, Hodijah, Maaseiah, Kelita, Azariah, Jozabad, Hanan, Pelaiah, and the Levites, caused the people to understand the law: and the people stood in their place. So they read in the book in the law of God distinctly, and gave the sense, and caused them to understand the reading.
>
> — Nehemiah 8:7–8

The Levites helped the people to understand the law of God, and the people became secure in their place in the land. They became stable as a result of gaining understanding. The Levites read in the book of the law of God *distinctly*, and gave the *sense* or meaning or policy or prosperity of the scripture. They helped the people to understand what was read. The Levites carried out a specific function to help the people become prosperous through understanding the Word of God that was spoken by the priests.

The scripture says, "So they read in the book of the law of God *distinctly* . . ." God gave me the brand **Distinguished Wisdom Present** . . . from this particular scripture. The Levites helped the people to *distinguish* what the Word of God was saying or what it really meant. The Webster's dictionary defines *distinguish* as "*to recognize plainly by any of the senses.*" The root meaning is *to prick or pierce apart*. The word *distinct* is defined as "*clearly marked off; plain; well defined; unmistakable.*" God used the Levites to clearly define His Word for the people so that it would be unmistakable what He meant. God wanted them to understand His true purpose for giving His laws, which is for our good.

When God gave me the brand and assignment for **Distinguished Wisdom Presents** . . . He indicated to me that he had anointed me to share wisdom in a *distinct* manner. Through my study of the book of Proverbs from childhood, I developed a love for wisdom and the Word of God. My education in communications helped to prepare me to speak God's Word. God gave me the name of the company Well Spoken Incorporated as a way of ministering His Word in a clear, specialized manner for those who needed to understand.

I began to share *Living Proverbs* as wisdom nuggets to friends and followers on social media as a means of spreading Gods Word to encourage, inspire, and inform. The platform of social media has allowed an expanded reach of God's Word into the world for both believers as well as secular society. God has a need for those who are willing to share his Word

Pastor Terrance Levise Turner, MBA

with the world. 2 Chronicles 15:3 indicate to us God's need for a *willing vessel* to share His Word. This is what it says,

> Now for a long season Israel hath been without the true God, and without a teaching priest, and without law.
>
> —2 Chronicles 15:3

God needs "*teaching priests*" who will teach His Word and bring understanding of His laws to society. This is my purpose, to fulfill God's *Great Commission* of spreading His Word and ways to the hearts of His people.

Please enjoy this book as a continual companion of counsel and guidance. All of the **Living Proverbs** are supported clearly by scriptural references. You will be able to have a relevant Bible study with every one of them. Your understanding of God's Word will increase as each layer of meaning is revealed from the scriptures used in this book. Meditate on them. Use it as a reference book. With every page you will find a *nugget* of wisdom that will enrich your daily life.

Now delve into the wisdom of God in **Distinguished Wisdom Presents . . . Living Proverbs–Vol. 5.** *May your life be enriched by the words of wisdom!*

—Pastor Terrance Levise Turner, MBA

Pastor Terrance Levise Turner, MBA

"Living Proverbs" –Vol. 5

2132. Wealth is about creating value. Wealth is not just about making money. If you only focus on making money, then, you're not building on solid ground. Money can be here today and gone tomorrow. However, if you create value, you can make money *all day long*.

Wilt thou set thine eyes upon that which is not? For riches certainly make themselves wings; they fly away as an eagle toward heaven.

Proverbs 23:5

2133. Don't forget to turn back your clock. This is a good time to turn over a new *leaf*. Let the old leaves fall away, and start a new habit. Let the old things pass away, and let new things come today.

Brethren, I count not myself to have apprehended: but this one thing I do, forgetting those things which are behind, and reaching forth unto those things which are before, I press toward the mark for the prize of the high calling of God in Christ Jesus.

Philippians 3:13-14

2134. Regarding weight management, it's not a matter of this meal or that pill. Rather, it's often simply a matter of the *treadmill*.

For bodily exercise profiteth little: but godliness is profitable unto all things, having promise of the life that now is, and of that which is to come.

1 Timothy 4:8

2135. Let your light so very much shine before people, because a lot of times favor has a lot to do with who sees you!

Seest thou a man diligent in his business? He shall stand before kings; he shall not stand before mean men.

Proverbs 22:29

2136. If you know who you are, and you know who your Heavenly Father is, then, you have to know that He controls the entire universe. He controls time and eternity. He controls the *flow of favor*. He has His hands on the steering wheel of your life. He controls the "GPS (*God's Positioning System*)." He can get you to where He's destined for you to be.

O the depth of the riches both of the wisdom and knowledge of God! How unsearchable are his judgments, and his ways past finding out! For who hath known the mind of the Lord? Or who hath been his counsellor? Or who hath first given to

him, and it shall be recompensed unto him again? For of him, and through him, and to him, are all things: to whom be glory forever. Amen.

Romans 11:33-36

2137. Practice loving yourself. Others will love you like *you* love you.

Jesus said unto him, thou shalt love the Lord thy God with all thy heart, and with all thy soul, and with all thy mind. This is the first and great commandment. And the second is like unto it, thou shalt love thy neighbour as thyself. On these two commandments hang all the law and the prophets.

Matthew 22:37-40

2138. Regarding love, the test of *time and trials* tells the true tale of love.

Charity suffereth long, and is kind; charity envieth not; charity vaunteth not itself, is not puffed up, doth not behave itself unseemly, seeketh not her own, is not easily provoked, thinketh no evil; rejoiceth not in iniquity, but rejoiceth in the truth; Beareth all things, believeth all things, hopeth all things, endureth all things. Charity never faileth: but whether there be prophecies, they shall fail; whether there be tongues, they shall cease; whether there be knowledge, it shall vanish away. For we know in part, and we prophesy in part. But when that which is perfect is come, then that which is in part shall be done away. When I was a child, I spake as a child, I

understood as a child, I thought as a child: but when I became a man, I put away childish things. For now we see through a glass, darkly; but then face to face: now I know in part; but then shall I know even as also I am known. And now abideth faith, hope, charity, these three; but the greatest of these is charity.

1 Corinthians 13:4-13

2139. The just shall live by faith, and not by *"fake"*. Speak what God's Word says, rather than, simply denying the facts. Confront the facts with the *truth*. Speak God's Word *only*, and you shall be healed, delivered, prospered, and made victorious. Live by faith, and not by *fake*. Live by the truth of God's Word.

Therefore it is of faith, that it might be by grace; to the end the promise might be sure to all the seed; not to that only which is of the law, but to that also which is of the faith of Abraham; who is the father of us all, (as it is written, I have made thee a father of many nations,) before him whom he believed, even God, who quickeneth the dead, and calleth those things which be not as though they were. Who against hope believed in hope, that he might become the father of many nations; according to that which was spoken, so shall thy seed be. And being not weak in faith, he considered not his own body now dead, when he was about an hundred years old, neither yet the deadness of Sara's womb.

Romans 4:16-19

2140. Pray anyway. Your problems may seem like a small thing in light of the big picture. But, remember, the big picture is made up of small things. Pray *anyway*.

And he spake a parable unto them *to this end*, that men ought always to pray, and not to faint.

> Luke 18:1

2141. An essential part of doing is *knowing*. Once you know what to do, you can do it. Make *knowing* a priority. An essential part of doing is *knowing*.

And that ye study to be quiet, and to do your own business, and to work with your own hands, as we commanded you; that ye may walk honestly toward them that are without, and that ye may have lack of nothing.

> 1 Thessalonians 4:11-12

2142. May God bless you with a *"one date relationship"*. A *wedding date* that will last for a lifetime!

And he answered and said unto them, have ye not read, that he which made them at the beginning made them male and female, and said, for this cause shall a man leave father and mother, and shall cleave to his wife: and they twain shall be one flesh? Wherefore they are no more twain, but one flesh. What therefore God hath joined together, let not man put asunder.

Matthew 19:4-6

2143. God isn't as interested in you living by miracles, as He is in you living by His *method*. He wants you to learn to live by His method, so that you can turn that wisdom over to your children and your children's children. Then, they can be free and never have to live in bondage again. Seek ye first the kingdom of God and His righteousness, and all these things shall be added unto you. Seek His wisdom. Seek His instruction. Seek His guidance. Seek His ways to success and prosperity. Live by His method, and not just by miracles.

And that ye study to be quiet, and to do your own business, and to work with your own hands, as we commanded you; that ye may walk honestly toward them that are without, and that ye may have lack of nothing.

1 Thessalonians 4:11-12

2144. Facts are relative. Truth is *timeless*. Build your life on the truth and you will be stable. You will endure the shifting facts of time.

For all flesh is as grass, and all the glory of man as the flower of grass. The grass withereth, and the flower thereof falleth away: but the word of the Lord endureth forever. And this is the word which by the gospel is preached unto you.

1 Peter 1:24-25

2145. Wages come from doing what you've *got* to do. Riches come from doing what you *get* to do.

Every man also to whom God hath given riches and wealth, and hath given him power to eat thereof, and to take his portion, and to rejoice in his labour; this is the gift of God. For he shall not much remember the days of his life; because God answereth him in the joy of his heart.

Ecclesiastes 5:19-20

2146. There's nothing wrong with not knowing. There's nothing wrong with not having experience. There's nothing wrong with not being sure as long as you're learning, and, as long as you're growing and increasing in pursuit of knowledge. Because, in time, you'll find out all that's necessary to successfully undertake whatever your challenge may be.

And that ye study to be quiet, and to do your own business, and to work with your own hands, as we commanded you; that ye may walk honestly toward them that are without, and that ye may have lack of nothing.

1 Thessalonians 4:11-12

2147. Success is a process. Profit takes time. However, if you don't go through the process, you'll never receive the profit.

For a dream cometh through the multitude of business; and a fool's voice is known by multitude of words.

>> Ecclesiastes 5:3

2148. Thank God for all the brave men and women that has served and is serving the United States Armed Forces. In God we trust, and on you we depend. Thank you for your service.

I exhort therefore, that, first of all, supplications, prayers, intercessions, and giving of thanks, be made for all men; for kings, and for all that are in authority; that we may lead a quiet and peaceable life in all godliness and honesty

>> 1 Timothy 2:1-2

2149. You only have one life to live. Therefore, *squeeze all the juice* that you can out of that lemon, and make lemonade! That way, you can also refresh the lives of others along the way. You have one life to live. Make the most of it!

There is that scattereth, and yet increaseth; and there is that withholdeth more than is meet, but it tendeth to poverty. The liberal soul shall be made fat: and he that watereth shall be watered also himself.

>> Proverbs 11:24-25

2150. You have to live your life like an *economist*. Don't be so moved by the ups and downs. Rather, watch the *trends*.

Let us hear the conclusion of the whole matter: fear God, and keep his commandments: for this is the whole duty of man. For God shall bring every work into judgment, with every secret thing, whether it be good, or whether it be evil.

Ecclesiastes 12:13-14

2151. As you mature in life, you should become more sober without becoming *sour*.

That the aged men be sober, grave, temperate, sound in faith, in charity, in patience. The aged women likewise, that they be in behaviour as becometh holiness, not false accusers, not given to much wine, teachers of good things; that they may teach the young women to be sober, to love their husbands, to love their children, to be discreet, chaste, keepers at home, good, obedient to their own husbands, that the word of God be not blasphemed. Young men likewise exhort to be sober minded.

Titus 2:2-6

2152. Why spend all of your time, energy, and years fighting to be a *slave*? When you can use that same time, energy, and years to fight to be *free*. Start that business. Study, partner, work, borrow if you have to, but by all means necessary, you can succeed, just like any of the companies you see out there that are succeeding. You are intelligent and capable to do what they've done and more. Extraordinary businesses are started and ran by ordinary people. You too have what it takes!

And that ye study to be quiet, and to do your own business, and to work with your own hands, as we commanded you; that ye may walk honestly toward them that are without, and that ye may have lack of nothing.

1 Thessalonians 4:11-12

2153. It's good to get outside consultation and help. However, always keep *the main thing* the main thing, and keep your *core* strong. For this is from where everything emanates. *You are* your source of wealth. Your wealth is released through your fellowship with Christ.

Abide in me, and I in you. As the branch cannot bear fruit of itself, except it abide in the vine; no more can ye, except ye abide in me. I am the vine, ye are the branches: he that abideth in me, and I in him, the same bringeth forth much fruit: for without me ye can do nothing.

John 15:4-5

2154. Don't be afraid. The same God that has been taking care of you all of these years is the same God that will continue to shelter you. Don't be afraid. Be wise. Be sober. Be watchful. Be prayerful. But, don't be afraid.

God is our refuge and strength, a very present help in trouble.

Psalm 46:1

2155. Regarding hard work, always take time to rest. Every *flow* needs to *ebb*.

And he said unto them, come ye yourselves apart into a desert place, and rest a while: for there were many coming and going, and they had no leisure so much as to eat.

Mark 6:31

2156. Regarding reputation, you have to prove yourself until you *prove yourself*. In spite of what you are already certain of about yourself. You still have to prove yourself until you prove yourself to others through your *results*.

But by the grace of God I am what I am: and his grace which *was bestowed* upon me was not in vain; but I laboured more abundantly than they all: yet not I, but the grace of God which was with me.

1 Corinthians 15:10

2157. Use what God gave you, to do what God made you to do, to get what God has for you.

For we are his workmanship, created in Christ Jesus unto good works, which God hath before ordained that we should walk in them.

Ephesians 2:10

2158. This is the season to give thanks for all that the Lord has done for us. Jesus died on the cross to pay for our sins. God, the Father, raised Jesus from the dead for our salvation and victory over sin, sickness, poverty, depression, and estrangement from God. Give Him thanks everyday!

It is a good thing to give thanks unto the Lord, and to sing praises unto thy name, O most high: to shew forth thy lovingkindness in the morning, and thy faithfulness every night.

> Psalm 92:1-2

2159. Regarding destiny, if you've done anything else, then, you can do *everything else* that's required for you to obtain your destiny!

I can do all things through Christ, which strengtheneth me.

> Philippians 4:13

2160. May God surround you with favor and His anointing like *seven layers of fat* protecting the core of your being.

For thou, Lord, wilt bless the righteous; with favour wilt thou compass him as with a shield.

> Psalm 5:12

2161. Christians without the fruit of the spirit are just as confusing to the world as *"Chamomile 5-hour Energy."*

Now the works of the flesh are manifest, which are these; adultery, fornication, uncleanness, lasciviousness, idolatry, witchcraft, hatred, variance, emulations, wrath, strife, seditions, heresies, envyings, murders, drunkenness, revellings, and such like: of the which I tell you before, as I have also told you in time past, that they which do such things shall not inherit the kingdom of God. But the fruit of the spirit is love, joy, peace, longsuffering, gentleness, goodness, faith, meekness, temperance: against such there is no law. And they that are Christ's have crucified the flesh with the affections and lusts. If we live in the spirit, let us also walk in the spirit.

Galatians 5:19-25

2162. Perfect faith casts out religion. Religion has torment.

There is no fear in love; but perfect love casteth out fear: because fear hath torment. He that feareth is not made perfect in love.

1 John 4:18

2163. Never neglect prayer and Bible study in order to give more time to work. One hour of dedicated prayer and Bible study will empower you for a full 12 hours of work. Always pray, because you never can tell what challenges a day may hold.

Now it came to pass, as they went, that he entered into a certain village: and a certain woman named Martha received him into her house. And she had a sister called Mary, which

also sat at Jesus' feet, and heard his word. But Martha was cumbered about much serving, and came to him, and said, Lord, dost thou not care that my sister hath left me to serve alone? Bid her therefore that she help me. And Jesus answered and said unto her, Martha, Martha, thou art careful and troubled about many things: but one thing is needful: and Mary hath chosen that good part, which shall not be taken away from her.

Luke 10:38-42

2164. Always take the time to pray. Sacrifice on the *front end* will prevent losses on the *back end*. Always acknowledge the Lord.

Trust in the Lord with all thine heart; and lean not unto thine own understanding. In all thy ways acknowledge him, and he shall direct thy paths.

Proverbs 3:5-6

2165. Concerning wisdom, sometimes you have to look pass the presentation in order to access the content.

And the same John had his raiment of camel's hair, and a leathern girdle about his loins; and his meat was locusts and wild honey. Then went out to him Jerusalem, and all Judaea, and all the region round about Jordan, and were baptized of him in Jordan, confessing their sins. But when he saw many of the Pharisees and Sadducees come to his baptism, he said unto them, O generation of vipers, who hath warned you to flee

from the wrath to come? Bring forth therefore fruits meet for repentance: and think not to say within yourselves, we have Abraham to our father: for I say unto you, that God is able of these stones to raise up children unto Abraham. And now also the axe is laid unto the root of the trees: therefore every tree, which bringeth not forth good fruit, is hewn down, and cast into the fire. I indeed baptize you with water unto repentance. But he that cometh after me is mightier than I, whose shoes I am not worthy to bear: he shall baptize you with the Holy Ghost, and with fire: whose fan is in his hand, and he will throughly purge his floor, and gather his wheat into the garner; but he will burn up the chaff with unquenchable fire.

Matthew 3:4-12

2166. Regarding how to become rich, the person who walks with wise people shall become wise. The person who walks with *rich* people shall become *rich*.

And lot also, which went with Abram, had flocks, and herds, and tents. And the land was not able to bear them, that they might dwell together: for their substance was great, so that they could not dwell together.

Genesis 13:5-6

2167. You don't need anyone else to *co-sign* on your destiny. If God gave it to you He is able to bring it to pass. He may use various people to contribute to your ultimate success, but always know that we are all only *actors* in God's great story. We are all a part of the making of *His-story*. If we will

simply play our roles and let God get the glory we will each receive our appropriate reward when the curtains drop in the end.

Not for that we have dominion over your faith, but are helpers of your joy: for by faith ye stand.

2 Corinthians 1:24

2168. There's a difference in having a conversation and receiving information from a hundred-thousandnaire or a millionaire compared to a *billionaire*. If you want to be a millionaire, then, you should receive information from a millionaire or a billionaire.

He that walketh with wise men shall be wise: but a companion of fools shall be destroyed.

Proverbs 13:20

2169. Receiving information from a billionaire increases the possibility of you becoming at least a *millionaire*.

And lot also, which went with Abram, had flocks, and herds, and tents. And the land was not able to bear them, that they might dwell together: for their substance was great, so that they could not dwell together.

Genesis 13:5-6

2170. God has "*chosen the foolish things of the world to confound the wise.*" However, He would prefer for each of us

to *wise up*! Then, He could get so much more of His will accomplished in the world through you.

Wisdom is good with an inheritance: and by it there is profit to them that see the sun. For wisdom is a defence, and money is a defence: but the excellency of knowledge is, that wisdom giveth life to them that have it.

Ecclesiastes 7:11-12

2171. The difference of being *godly correct*, rather than, just politically correct, can determine eternal direction.

There are many devices in a man's heart; nevertheless the counsel of the Lord, that shall stand.

Proverbs 19:21

2172. Train up a child in the way that he or she should go, and when he or she is old, he or she will not depart from it. No matter which way the wind may blow the tree, at least he or she will have roots. No matter how the ship may sway on the sea of life, at least he or she will have an anchor.

And the Lord said, shall I hide from Abraham that thing which I do; seeing that Abraham shall surely become a great and mighty nation, and all the nations of the earth shall be blessed in him? For I know him, that he will command his children and his household after him, and they shall keep the way of the Lord, to do justice and judgment; that the Lord may bring upon Abraham that which he hath spoken of him.

Genesis 18:17-19

2173. Faith is taking action on what you hope for. Action is the evidence that you believe what you do not see. Action is the only thing that gives substance to the dream you talk about.

For a dream cometh through the multitude of business; and a fool's voice is known by multitude of words.

Ecclesiastes 5:3

2174. You should seek the blessing that God promises to every person who worships and reverences Him. God desires for you to profit from the labor of your own hands. He desires for you to be happy in life. He desires for you to have a successful, fruitful family life, and to live a long, healthy life. God desires for you to see your children's children and to see prosperity in your family from generation to generation. This is the promise and blessing of the Lord that you should pursue. It takes effort, but you should pursue it. You can accomplish it.

Blessed is every one that feareth the Lord; that walketh in his ways. For thou shalt eat the labour of thine hands: happy shalt thou be, and it shall be well with thee. Thy wife shall be as a fruitful vine by the sides of thine house: thy children like olive plants round about thy table. Behold, that thus shall the man be blessed that feareth the Lord. The Lord shall bless thee out of Zion: and thou shalt see the good of Jerusalem all the days

of thy life. Yea, thou shalt see thy children's children, and peace upon Israel.

Psalm 128

2175. Regarding relationships, maintenance is so much better than repair or replacement, especially for those things that are irreplaceable.

It is a snare to the man who devoureth that which is holy, and after vows to make enquiry.

Proverbs 20:25

2176. In regard to balance, you can't do everything all of the time, but you can do some of the things some of the time. Prioritization is the key.

Say not ye, there are yet four months, and then cometh harvest? Behold, I say unto you, lift up your eyes, and look on the fields; for they are white already to harvest.

John 4:35

2177. Economics is the great equalizer. Applied knowledge is the key to economic strength, power, growth, and stability.

And that ye study to be quiet, and to do your own business, and to work with your own hands, as we commanded you; that ye may walk honestly toward them that are without, and that ye may have lack of nothing.

1 Thessalonians 4:11-12

2178. Don't be intimidated by fear pressure or peer pressure.

But none of these things move me, neither count I my life dear unto myself, so that I might finish my course with joy, and the ministry, which I have received of the Lord Jesus, to testify the gospel of the grace of God.

Acts 20:24

2179. In regard to the new place that God has called you into, even though it may have problems, remember, He didn't call you there because it was already ok. He called you there to be a *change agent*. You are the light of the world. Let your light so very much shine before the world, so that you drive out the darkness.

Ye are the salt of the earth: but if the salt have lost his savour, wherewith shall it be salted? It is thenceforth good for nothing, but to be cast out, and to be trodden under foot of men. Ye are the light of the world. A city that is set on an hill cannot be hid. Neither do men light a candle, and put it under a bushel, but on a candlestick; and it giveth light unto all that are in the house. Let your light so shine before men, that they may see your good works, and glorify your father which is in heaven.

Matthew 5:13-16

2180. If we truly walk in love we will forgive. If we truly walk in love there will be less reasons to forgive.

If ye fulfil the royal law according to the scripture, thou shalt love thy neighbour as thyself, ye do well.

James 2:8

2181. Engineers figure things out. They figure things out even when they don't have all of the instructions or pieces. They take what they have to solve the problem at hand. Life has provided us with problems and opportunities. Sometimes we don't have all of the instructions. However, we do have the basic elements for the pieces. Whatever your problem may be, there's an answer. Research, study, test, and try, because there is an answer. Engineers figure things out.

If any of you lack wisdom, let him ask of God, that giveth to all men liberally, and upbraideth not; and it shall be given him.

James 1:5

2182. Always strive to do what you do in excellence. Excellence attracts excellence. Mediocrity repels excellence. People of excellence like to work with excellent people.

Seest thou a man diligent in his business? He shall stand before kings; he shall not stand before mean men.

Proverbs 22:29

2183. Regarding the journey toward your destiny, learn to enjoy the blessings during the ride to your destination, and you will better appreciate it when you have arrived.

Behold that which I have seen: it is good and comely for one to eat and to drink, and to enjoy the good of all his labour that he taketh under the sun all the days of his life, which God giveth him: for it is his portion. Every man also to whom God hath given riches and wealth, and hath given him power to eat thereof, and to take his portion, and to rejoice in his labour; this is the gift of God. For he shall not much remember the days of his life; because God answereth him in the joy of his heart.

Ecclesiastes 5:18-20

2184. For God not to come through on His Word after that you have done everything that He told you to do in His Word, would be like the Sun not rising in the morning, the cold not coming in the Winter, the heat not coming in the Summer, the flowers not blooming in the Spring, or the crop not coming during Harvest. If you have planted the seeds of obedience to God's Word, then, you can be assured of a harvest as sure as the Heavens and Earth remain.

Heaven and earth shall pass away: but my words shall not pass away.

Mark 13:31

2185. If the miracle that you have been believing God for has been taking some time, then, it is just God giving you time to learn to live by His principles. Miracles happen sometimes. However, if you learn the principles, you can make miracles happen *anytime* and all the time, and you can pass the principles down-line to the next generation.

And the Lord said, shall I hide from Abraham that thing which I do; seeing that Abraham shall surely become a great and mighty nation, and all the nations of the earth shall be blessed in him? For I know him, that he will command his children and his household after him, and they shall keep the way of the Lord, to do justice and judgment; that the Lord may bring upon Abraham that which he hath spoken of him.

Genesis 18:17-19

2186. In a country, many times the definition of justice is determined by whoever is currently in power. Typically, the definition of justice will be skewed according to whether it advantages or pleases the current administration or particular *powers that be* during the specified era.

If thou seest the oppression of the poor, and violent perverting of judgment and justice in a province, marvel not at the matter: for he that is higher than the highest regardeth; and there be higher than they.

Ecclesiastes 5:8

2187. Rather than being as shocked by all of the *shocking* videos of people doing *shocking* things when they think no one else is looking, we should be *shocked* by the fact that wherever you go there are hidden video cameras to record your every move. We should be *shocked* that this has become expected and acceptable. We should be *shocked* by how we have welcomed the relinquishing of our privacy as free citizens.

If thou seest the oppression of the poor, and violent perverting of judgment and justice in a province, marvel not at the matter: for he that is higher than the highest regardeth; and there be higher than they.

Ecclesiastes 5:8

2188. Marriage should be about going forward, doing things, accomplishing goals, and capturing dreams!

Now when the turn of Esther, the daughter of Abigail the uncle of Mordecai, who had taken her for his daughter, was come to go in unto the king, she required nothing but what Hegai the king's chamberlain, the keeper of the women, appointed. And Esther obtained favour in the sight of all them that looked upon her. So Esther was taken unto king Ahasuerus into his house royal in the tenth month, which is the month Tebeth, in the seventh year of his reign. And the king loved Esther above all the women, and she obtained grace and favour in his sight more than all the virgins; so that he set the royal crown upon her head, and made her queen instead of Vashti. Then the king made a great feast unto all his

princes and his servants, even Esther's feast; and he made a release to the provinces, and gave gifts, according to the state of the king.

Esther 2:15-18

2189. Regarding readiness, it's good to be "*instant in season and out of season*", even if you have to wear a coat. In other words, be ready to take advantage of opportunities, even if you have to make adjustments to do so.

Whatsoever thy hand findeth to do, do it with thy might; for there is no work, nor device, nor knowledge, nor wisdom, in the grave, whither thou goest. I returned, and saw under the sun, that the race is not to the swift, nor the battle to the strong, neither yet bread to the wise, nor yet riches to men of understanding, nor yet favour to men of skill; but time and chance happeneth to them all.

Ecclesiastes 9:10-11

2190. God is a mastermind, even when you can't *master* His mind. You may not understand all of the details of His plan, but that doesn't prove that He doesn't have a plan. He does have a plan for your life, and it's good! He has plans for you to have a prosperous and peaceful outcome. He is masterful at getting His children to His desired outcome for them.

For I know the thoughts that I think toward you, saith the Lord, thoughts of peace, and not of evil, to give you an expected end.

Jeremiah 29:11

2191. Pay off your small credit cards as soon as possible, because the *small foxes* spoil the credit!

Take us the foxes, the little foxes, that spoil the vines: for our vines have tender grapes.

Song of Solomon 2:15

2192. Not every door is an automatic door. Sometimes you have to *push*.

For a great door and effectual is opened unto me, and there are many adversaries.

1 Corinthians 16:9

2193. Regarding productivity, the sign of your gratefulness for God's opportunities in your life is your determined, productive use of your time, talents, and resources. Your results are your greatest praise for the life He's given you. You and I will be rewarded in life, and in heaven, for our results during our lifetime.

For the kingdom of heaven is as a man travelling into a far country, who called his own servants, and delivered unto them his goods. And unto one he gave five talents, to another two, and to another one; to every man according to his several ability; and straightway took his journey. Then he that had received the five talents went and traded with the same, and

made them other five talents. And likewise he that had received two, he also gained other two. But he that had received one went and digged in the earth, and hid his Lord's money. After a long time the Lord of those servants cometh, and reckoneth with them. And so he that had received five talents came and brought other five talents, saying, Lord, thou deliveredst unto me five talents: behold, I have gained beside them five talents more. His Lord said unto him, well done, thou good and faithful servant: thou hast been faithful over a few things, I will make thee ruler over many things: enter thou into the joy of thy Lord. He also that had received two talents came and said, Lord, thou deliveredst unto me two talents: behold, I have gained two other talents beside them. His Lord said unto him, well done, good and faithful servant; thou hast been faithful over a few things, I will make thee ruler over many things: enter thou into the joy of thy Lord. Then he which had received the one talent came and said, Lord, I knew thee that thou art an hard man, reaping where thou hast not sown, and gathering where thou hast not strawed: and I was afraid, and went and hid thy talent in the earth: lo, there thou hast that is thine. His Lord answered and said unto him, thou wicked and slothful servant, thou knewest that I reap where I sowed not, and gather where I have not strawed: thou oughtest therefore to have put my money to the exchangers, and then at my coming I should have received mine own with usury. Take therefore the talent from him, and give it unto him which hath ten talents. For unto every one that hath shall be given, and he shall have abundance: but from him that hath not shall be taken away even that which he hath.

Matthew 25:14-29

2194. Regarding critics of your *success schedule*, people who haven't sown any seed toward your success, have no right to evaluate your success schedule. Your ultimate success is between your own efforts and God's divine favor.

But let every man prove his own work, and then shall he have rejoicing in himself alone, and not in another.

Galatians 6:4

2195. Regarding your creative preferences, be sure to meet your own personal standards of excellence and taste. Then, every other opinion will be only commentary. Always present your best in excellence, and let public taste bend to you through your successful marketing of the benefits of your products and services.

Prepare thy work without, and make it fit for thyself in the field; and afterwards build thine house.

Proverbs 24:27

2196. I'm not done, until I'm *rich!*

The crown of the wise is their riches: but the foolishness of fools is folly.

Proverbs 14:24

2197. Some people fight to be poor, because they don't have the faith to be rich.

The crown of the wise is their riches: but the foolishness of fools is folly.

Proverbs 14:24

2198. Often we say "Somebody aught to do something". Yet, we often are complaining with the solution in *our* mouth. Rather than complain, we should be like the enthusiastic student in school, and step up to the *chalkboard of life* and solve the problem.

But what saith it? The word is nigh thee, even in thy mouth, and in thy heart: that is, the word of faith, which we preach; that if thou shalt confess with thy mouth the Lord Jesus, and shalt believe in thine heart that God hath raised him from the dead, thou shalt be saved. For with the heart man believeth unto righteousness; and with the mouth confession is made unto salvation. For the scripture saith, whosoever believeth on him shall not be ashamed. For there is no difference between the Jew and the Greek: for the same Lord over all is rich unto all that call upon him. For whosoever shall call upon the name of the Lord shall be saved.

Romans 10:8-13

2199. Use criticism as fuel to help you keep going as quickly as possible in the right direction.

Shew me a token for good; that they which hate me may see it, and be ashamed: because thou, Lord, hast holpen me, and comforted me.

>   Psalm 86:17

2200. Sometimes the dream must bow to the wakened eye. Though the dream may sleep, never let the dream die. Though your hope may be deferred, your heart still beats. If you keep arising up, the dream will be complete.

Hope deferred maketh the heart sick: but when the desire cometh, it is a tree of life.

>   Proverbs 13:12

2201. Go forward and trust God that you're going to reach your destination. Don't worry. Stay busy. You will be much happier.

Now faith is the substance of things hoped for, the evidence of things not seen. For by it the elders obtained a good report.

>   Hebrews 11:1-2

2202. Chickens gather in a crowd, but eagles travel alone. Don't be afraid of alone time. God is giving you time to discover and refine your *distinction*. Chickens gather in a crowd, but eagles travel alone.

Through desire a man, having separated himself, seeketh and intermeddleth with all wisdom.

Proverbs 18:1

2203. The more money that you make, the less you talk. The more money that you make, the less you have to convince people in order for you to *make* money. Money comes from *results*.

In all labour there is profit: but the talk of the lips tendeth only to penury.

Proverbs 14:23

2204. One of the best keys to self-motivation is *self-congratulation*. Congratulate yourself on what you've already accomplished, and you will be motivated to do more!

That the communication of thy faith may become effectual by the acknowledging of every good thing which is in you in Christ Jesus.

Philemon 1:6

2205. One of the greatest things that you can do is to learn to *think for yourself*. That will set you free from being held hostage to the opinions of others.

But let every man prove his own work, and then shall he have rejoicing in himself alone, and not in another.

Galatians 6:4

2206. The strength of society is built upon the manipulation of others. Your liberty is built upon the liberation of your own individual life and dreams.

Then said Jesus to those Jews which believed on him, if ye continue in my word, then are ye my disciples indeed; and ye shall know the truth, and the truth shall make you free.

John 8:31-32

2207. In regard to goal attainment, any progress is good.

In all labour there is profit: but the talk of the lips tendeth only to penury.

Proverbs 14:23

2208. You are an *event* that is happening upon Earth that will shape the future of the world.

For if thou altogether holdest thy peace at this time, then shall there enlargement and deliverance arise to the Jews from another place; but thou and thy father's house shall be destroyed: and who knoweth whether thou art come to the kingdom for such a time as this?

Esther 4:14

2209. The key to peace during progress is *one day at a time*, *one person at a time*, and *one decision at a time*.

The steps of a good man are ordered by the Lord: and he delighteth in his way.

Psalm 37:23

2210. Revolutionary change and progress has always occurred at the intersection of religion and *revelation*. Whether it was through the introduction of the ministry of Jesus Christ, the Apostle Paul, or Martin Luther. However, the future of culture and the world has always depended upon the messengers of God's will for *"such a time as this."*

For if thou altogether holdest thy peace at this time, then shall there enlargement and deliverance arise to the Jews from another place; but thou and thy father's house shall be destroyed: and who knoweth whether thou art come to the kingdom for such a time as this?

Esther 4:14

2211. Your personal insecurities and the insecurities and envy of others will be your greatest challenges to overcome in your fight for your dream. However, as you overcome the former, you will simultaneously overcome the latter. No one can truly claim your success, but you. Once you come into your fullest, truest self, no adversary can block you. You will become truly *unstoppable!*

For your shame ye shall have double; and for confusion they shall rejoice in their portion: therefore in their land they shall possess the double: everlasting joy shall be unto them.

Isaiah 61:7

2212. There are two kinds of assets: financial assets and real assets. Financial assets are based on the existence of real assets. Financial assets include stocks, bonds, options, and derivatives, etc. Whereas, real assets include land, buildings, houses, equipment, and labor. Therefore, you want to take time to invest in real assets, while also understanding financial assets when it comes to managing the money that is made from your real assets. However, you want to make sure that you invest in, own, and manage real assets, such as houses, land, buildings, equipment, labor, and time.

I love them that love me; and those that seek me early shall find me. Riches and honour are with me; yea, durable riches and righteousness. My fruit is better than gold, yea, than fine gold; and my revenue than choice silver. I lead in the way of righteousness, in the midst of the paths of judgment: that I may cause those that love me to inherit substance; and I will fill their treasures.

Proverbs 8:17-21

2213. Everyone is a star in someone else's sky, so shine while you can. Make the most of your days and nights. Shine as bright as the Sun in the day. Give direction and guidance as the North Star in someone's night. Let your light so very much shine! You are the *star* in someone else's sky!

Ye are the salt of the earth: but if the salt have lost his savour, wherewith shall it be salted? It is thenceforth good for

nothing, but to be cast out, and to be trodden under foot of men. Ye are the light of the world. A city that is set on an hill cannot be hid. Neither do men light a candle, and put it under a bushel, but on a candlestick; and it giveth light unto all that are in the house. Let your light so shine before men, that they may see your good works, and glorify your father which is in heaven.

Matthew 5:13-16

2214. Anything that's out of order will eventually break down. Take time to fix your life. Get it straight, because if anything is out of order it will eventually break down.

Let all things be done decently and in order.

1 Corinthians 14:40

2215. Workers get paid by the hour. Producers get paid by the product. Workers earn a wage. Producers earn wealth.

The crown of the wise is their riches: but the foolishness of fools is folly.

Proverbs 14:24

2216. Balance is the key to avoiding neglect. If you do all that you need to do in balance, you will avoid neglecting to do all that you need to do.

Let all things be done decently and in order.

1 Corinthians 14:40

2217. Gold, silver, precious stones, and the *anointing* do not depreciate in value overtime. Each will enrich your life. Each is an inheritance. The anointing will bring healing and prosperity to your life.

There is treasure to be desired and oil in the dwelling of the wise; but a foolish man spendeth it up.

Proverbs 21:20

2218. Regarding achieving the destination of success, ignorance of where you're going, and lack of knowledge regarding how to get there, makes achieving the destination seem so far away. However, once you ask someone who has already arrived at the destination of success for the exact directions, the journey becomes shorter and less daunting. Get wisdom. Get understanding. It will make your trip faster and more enjoyable.

Without counsel purposes are disappointed: but in the multitude of counsellors they are established.

Proverbs 15:22

2219. We're all subject to prayer.

I exhort therefore, that, first of all, supplications, prayers, intercessions, and giving of thanks, be made for all men; for

kings, and for all that are in authority; that we may lead a quiet and peaceable life in all godliness and honesty.

1 Timothy 2:1-2

2220. The good that you do today is a down payment on tomorrow's blessings.

Be not deceived; God is not mocked: for whatsoever a man soweth, that shall he also reap. For he that soweth to his flesh shall of the flesh reap corruption; but he that soweth to the spirit shall of the spirit reap life everlasting. And let us not be weary in well doing: for in due season we shall reap, if we faint not. As we have therefore opportunity, let us do good unto all men, especially unto them who are of the household of faith.

Galatians 6:7-10

2221. Do your best as you work on the job today. Serve well. Make a difference. Enrich the lives of others. Furthermore, be sure to work on your own business and mind. The work that you do on your own business and mind will be the key to continual enrichment.

And that ye study to be quiet, and to do your own business, and to work with your own hands, as we commanded you; that ye may walk honestly toward them that are without, and that ye may have lack of nothing.

1 Thessalonians 4:11-12

2222. As saints of God, of course it's our ultimate goal to hear Jesus say "Well done". However, we also should want to live here long enough to give Him something to say, "Well done" about.

He said therefore, a certain nobleman went into a far country to receive for himself a kingdom, and to return. And he called his ten servants, and delivered them ten pounds, and said unto them, Occupy till I come.

Luke 19:12-13

2223. In regard to success, God gives you time to realize who you are. You go through various trials, tests, challenges, and growth processes to learn who you are, what you have, what you can do, and what you can become. God gives you an opportunity to realize your own strengths and your own abilities. He allows you to realize that through Him, you can do all things through Christ, which strengthens you.

I can do all things through Christ, which strengtheneth me.

Philippians 4:13

2224. Keep on praying. Keep on doing. Everything is going to be alright!

Even so faith, if it hath not works, is dead, being alone. Yea, a man may say, thou hast faith, and I have works: shew me thy faith without thy works, and I will shew thee my faith by my works.

James 2:17-18

2225. You are the *dictionary*. You have extracted *meaning* out of life. People should be able to look to you to determine the definition of what's right or wrong.

Do we begin again to commend ourselves? Or need we, as some others, epistles of commendation to you, or letters of commendation from you? Ye are our epistle written in our hearts, known and read of all men: Forasmuch as ye are manifestly declared to be the epistle of Christ ministered by us, written not with ink, but with the spirit of the living God; not in tables of stone, but in fleshy tables of the heart.

2 Corinthians 3:1-3

2226. Always invest good seed into your children, because that's what they will reach back for when they become adults. They will build the future upon the *sure stones* that you lay along the path of their growing up years.

Remove not the ancient landmark, which thy fathers have set.

Proverbs 22:28

2227. If you have a *product*, then, you have a *promise* that if you *pursue* you will have a *profit*.

In all labour there is profit: but the talk of the lips tendeth only to penury.

> Proverbs 14:23

2228. Success takes time, but if you take the time you will succeed.

The steps of a good man are ordered by the Lord: and he delighteth in his way.

> Psalm 37:23

2229. Regarding life and happiness, you have to peel off the rinds, spit out the seeds, and squeeze all of the juice that you can out of life. After awhile you'll realize that even the rinds can become fertilizer to grow the seeds that you spit out along the way.

In the morning sow thy seed, and in the evening withhold not thine hand: for thou knowest not whether shall prosper, either this or that, or whether they both shall be alike good.

> Ecclesiastes 11:6

2230. In regard to production, go quick on art, slow on construction. One you must capture the beauty before it passes, the other must be built to last. According to the skill of the artist or the construction worker, the work could be timeless.

According to the grace of God which is given unto me, as a wise masterbuilder, I have laid the foundation, and another

buildeth thereon. But let every man take heed how he buildeth thereupon.

1 Corinthians 3:10

2231. The *spirit of faith* is completely unbiased. Whosoever is exposed to it will receive the benefits, if he or she would only act upon it!

We having the same spirit of faith, according as it is written, I believed, and therefore have I spoken; we also believe, and therefore speak.

2 Corinthians 4:13

2232. God's eyes are *"running to and fro"* throughout the earth, looking for someone to bless. Give Him something to bless by obeying His commandment to be fruitful, creative, and productive. His angels are informing Him of those who are at the peak of ripeness for a blessing! Let that be you!

For the eyes of the Lord run to and fro throughout the whole earth, to shew himself strong in the behalf of them whose heart is perfect toward him . . .

2 Chronicles 16:9a

2233. Not all of the Bible is about being *"sweet, warm, and fuzzy"*. Much of the "warm and fuzzy" has been preached to control and subjugate an enslaved people, whether in the Roman Empire or in the United States of America. However,

the true Gospel of the Bible is about deliverance from slavery, poverty, and oppression. The true Gospel is about possessing the promises of God.

The spirit of the Lord is upon me, because he hath anointed me to preach the gospel to the poor; he hath sent me to heal the brokenhearted, to preach deliverance to the captives, and recovering of sight to the blind, to set at liberty them that are bruised, To preach the acceptable year of the Lord.

Luke 4:18-19

2234. Here is a mystery of faith: Stretch out farther than you can comfortably see, and God will take you further than where you may have gone at first. Your courage to *stretch* licenses God to take you to the next level.

Enlarge the place of thy tent, and let them stretch forth the curtains of thine habitations: spare not, lengthen thy cords, and strengthen thy stakes; for thou shalt break forth on the right hand and on the left; and thy seed shall inherit the Gentiles, and make the desolate cities to be inhabited.

Isaiah 54:2-3

2235. "Dear Heavenly Father, help me to clearly discern and courageously assume my responsibilities today with joy. Thank you for your grace to do all things that I need to do, through the effectual, abiding presence of the Lord Jesus Christ within me. Help me to continually lean in upon the abundant supply of your Spirit within me through a confident,

continued inner prayer-life and communion with you today. In Jesus name, amen."

Abide in me, and I in you. As the branch cannot bear fruit of itself, except it abide in the vine; no more can ye, except ye abide in me. I am the vine, ye are the branches: he that abideth in me, and I in him, the same bringeth forth much fruit: for without me ye can do nothing.

John 15:4-5

2236. Totally depend upon the grace of God today.

Yet the Lord will command his lovingkindness in the day time, and in the night his song shall be with me, and my prayer unto the God of my life.

Psalm 42:8

2237. The key to having an advantage in life is to have choices. The key to maximizing choices is to *focus*. Just like in college . . . it's a great advantage to have all kinds of positive choices and opportunities. However, the most successful student is the one who has the discernment to focus on what he or she truly wants and to go for it with all of his or her heart. Choices are an advantage. Yet, *focus* is the key to maximizing that advantage.

My son, attend to my words; incline thine ear unto my sayings. Let them not depart from thine eyes; keep them in the midst of thine heart. For they are life unto those that find

them, and health to all their flesh. Keep thy heart with all diligence; for out of it are the issues of life. Put away from thee a froward mouth, and perverse lips put far from thee. Let thine eyes look right on, and let thine eyelids look straight before thee. Ponder the path of thy feet, and let all thy ways be established. Turn not to the right hand nor to the left: remove thy foot from evil.

Proverbs 4:20-27

2238. Don't let limited thinkers limit your dream. Most people have mediocre ability to think *outside of the box* of their own experiences and expectations for themselves. When they come in close contact with an exceptional dreamer, they enviously attempt to minimize, limit, and sabotage the measure of the dreamer's vision for themselves. *Run!* Escape the grasp of dream killers! God will move you into an environment where your dream can thrive, even if it takes adversity to get you there. Your dream is your collaboration with God. It will serve many people.

And Joseph dreamed a dream, and he told it his brethren: and they hated him yet the more. And he said unto them, hear, I pray you, this dream which I have dreamed: for, behold, we were binding sheaves in the field, and, lo, my sheaf arose, and also stood upright; and, behold, your sheaves stood round about, and made obeisance to my sheaf. And his brethren said to him, shalt thou indeed reign over us? Or shalt thou indeed have dominion over us? And they hated him yet the more for his dreams, and for his words. And he dreamed yet another dream, and told it his brethren, and said, behold, I have

dreamed a dream more; and, behold, the sun and the moon and the eleven stars made obeisance to me. And he told it to his father, and to his brethren: and his father rebuked him, and said unto him, what is this dream that thou hast dreamed? Shall I and thy mother and thy brethren indeed come to bow down ourselves to thee to the earth? And his brethren envied him; but his father observed the saying.

Genesis 37:5-11

2239. Believe in the Lord through learning His Word and ways in the Bible. Go to church and listen to preaching. Study the Bible. Pray. Furthermore, obey what the Bible instructs, by listening to and learning from those who have become *profitable* through God's principles. The true *prophets* of God are those who have become *profitable* through God's principles, and have dedicated their lives to teaching others what they've learned, so that others can become profitable too.

And they rose early in the morning, and went forth into the wilderness of Tekoa: and as they went forth, Jehoshaphat stood and said, hear me, O Judah, and ye inhabitants of Jerusalem; believe in the Lord your God, so shall ye be established; believe his prophets, so shall ye prosper.

2 Chronicles 20:20

2240. You are a fully-fledged success! Therefore, *soar*! The definition of *"fledged"* is *"to grow the feathers needed to fly."* You have everything you need now to reach the highest

heights of success. You can overcome any rough currents of life. You truly are a *fully-fledged* success. Now, *soar*!

But they that wait upon the Lord shall renew their strength; they shall mount up with wings as eagles; they shall run, and not be weary; and they shall walk, and not faint.

Isaiah 40:31

2241. Inspiration, impartation, and instruction are the keys to promotion and obtaining your destiny.

All scripture is given by inspiration of God, and is profitable for doctrine, for reproof, for correction, for instruction in righteousness.

2 Timothy 3:16

2242. Everyone has his or her own particular style. Everyone has his or her own particular advantages. Everyone has his or her own particular gifts. There's never any reason to be jealous of another person. There's never any reason to be envious of another person. Just be exceptional on your level.

As every man hath received the gift, even so minister the same one to another, as good stewards of the manifold grace of God.

1 Peter 4:10

2243. Don't be problem oriented. Be solution oriented. The problem is in the past. The solution is in the future.

Brethren, I count not myself to have apprehended: but this one thing I do, forgetting those things which are behind, and reaching forth unto those things which are before, I press toward the mark for the prize of the high calling of God in Christ Jesus.

Philippians 3:13-14

2244. Regarding problems and priorities, if you solved the most immediate problem that you needed to solve today, then, you solved the problem that you needed to solve for today.

Boast not thyself of to morrow; for thou knowest not what a day may bring forth.

Proverbs 27:1

2245. People who become legendary were already *"legends in their own minds"*, and that's how they became legendary.

For as he thinketh in his heart, so is he...

Proverbs 23:7a

2246. Hope you're having a blessed Christmas evening. Are you watching Christmas movies? The best is ahead. God is faithful. He's been faithful in the past. He will fulfill His promises to us. The best is coming your way in the New Year! Be encouraged about your future. You will be pleasantly

surprised at how many blessings God has in store for you and your family. Merry Christmas!

For unto you is born this day in the city of David a saviour, which is Christ the Lord. And this *shall be a* sign unto you; ye shall find the babe wrapped in swaddling clothes, lying in a manger. And suddenly there was with the angel a multitude of the heavenly host praising God, and saying, glory to God in the highest, and on earth peace, good will toward men.

Luke 2:11-14

2247. Everybody has the opportunity to become great, if they will only take the opportunity, and make the most of it.

Whatsoever thy hand findeth to do, do it with thy might; for there is no work, nor device, nor knowledge, nor wisdom, in the grave, whither thou goest. I returned, and saw under the sun, that the race is not to the swift, nor the battle to the strong, neither yet bread to the wise, nor yet riches to men of understanding, nor yet favour to men of skill; but time and chance happeneth to them all.

Ecclesiastes 9:10-11

2248. This New Year you will prosper by the *anointing*. It won't be by your own ingenuity. It will be by God's anointing. It's not by might, nor by power, but by God's anointing that you will prosper this New Year! Stay connected to the source of your strength and prosperity, the Lord Jesus Christ. Maintain a vibrant, dependent prayer-life. Stay in God's Word

by reading the Bible. Worship God daily with singing. The anointing will flow in all that you do this New Year!

For the eyes of the Lord run to and fro throughout the whole earth, to shew himself strong in the behalf of them whose heart is perfect toward him...

2 Chronicles 16:9a

2249. The key to your success and progress in the New Year will be your *passion*! Keep yourself motivated by continually feeding your faith with inspiring words and experiences. Keep sparking your faith, and you will stay ignited for success and progress in this New Year!

Behold, all ye that kindle a fire, that compass yourselves about with sparks: walk in the light of your fire, and in the sparks that ye have kindled ...

Isaiah 50:11a

2250. Learn what you need to learn in order to earn what you want from the Lord, so that when you receive it, no one can act like they gave you a favor. Rather, you took the time to study and invest what was required in order to obtain what God has always wanted you to have. So that, at the end of the day, all that you will be required to say is, "Thank you Lord for fulfilling your Word unto me!"

And that ye study to be quiet, and to do your own business, and to work with your own hands, as we commanded you;

that ye may walk honestly toward them that are without, and that ye may have lack of nothing.

1 Thessalonians 4:11-12

2251. *Everybody* is living by faith. Business owners, entrepreneurs, farmers, etc., are all living by faith. So, if you're disappointed about living by faith, you'll never get a big harvest. It takes faith. It takes stretching in order to get a harvest. You have to be willing to take risks on what you do not see, so that you can see what you do not see.

But without faith it is impossible to please him: for he that cometh to God must believe that he is, and that he is a rewarder of them that diligently seek him.

Hebrews 11:6

2252. How do you win the day in this New Year? By simple diligence, productivity, and persistence.

There be four things which are little upon the earth, but they are exceeding wise: The ants are a people not strong, yet they prepare their meat in the summer; The conies are but a feeble folk, yet make they their houses in the rocks; The locusts have no king, yet go they forth all of them by bands; The spider taketh hold with her hands, and is in kings' palaces.

Proverbs 30:24-28

2253. Life is "pay-to-play." Consequently, it *pays to play*. Go to college. Go to seminars. Go to conferences. Buy and read books. Join trade associations. Get into training programs. Life is "pay to play". However, it *pays to play*.

Buy the truth, and sell it not; also wisdom, and instruction, and understanding.

Proverbs 23:23

2254. You are important. However, your realization of your importance is what's so important to all the people that are depending on you. You are significant. You are important. So, *be important*.

That the communication of thy faith may become effectual by the acknowledging of every good thing which is in you in Christ Jesus.

Philemon 1:6

2255. Don't try to be politically correct. Strive to be *biblically* correct. Because, being biblically correct will stand the test of time.

There are many devices in a man's heart; nevertheless the counsel of the Lord, that shall stand.

Proverbs 19:21

2256. As a Christian, if you get into a flesh fight, you will lose every time, because you have to operate in your spiritual authority in order to truly have victory in life. Our place of victory is in the spirit realm, based on the blood of Jesus. We cannot walk by the flesh. We have to walk by the spirit. We must walk after the spirit, and not after the flesh. It's through this that we have total victory. No weapon formed against us can prosper, and every lying tongue that rises up against us in judgment, we shall condemn. This is the heritage of the servants of the Lord. How much more for us as sons and daughters of the Most High God, and our righteousness is of the Lord.

For though we walk in the flesh, we do not war after the flesh: (for the weapons of our warfare are not carnal, but mighty through God to the pulling down of strong holds;) casting down imaginations, and every high thing that exalteth itself against the knowledge of God, and bringing into captivity every thought to the obedience of Christ.

2 Corinthians 10:3-5

2257. One day, my mother and I were driving down the street and we looked over and saw a piece of property that had been cleared out, and we looked at each other and said, "What was there? I don't even remember what was there!" That's a lesson for each of us. You don't want your life to be so insignificant, in regard to impact, that when you're gone people don't even remember what you did or what you were about. You want to live so that you make an impact, so that you're remembered when you're gone.

Pastor Terrance Levise Turner, MBA

For to him that is joined to all the living there is hope: for a living dog is better than a dead lion. For the living know that they shall die: but the dead know not any thing, neither have they any more a reward; for the memory of them is forgotten. Also their love, and their hatred, and their envy, is now perished; neither have they any more a portion for ever in any thing that is done under the sun. Go thy way, eat thy bread with joy, and drink thy wine with a merry heart; for God now accepteth thy works. Let thy garments be always white; and let thy head lack no ointment. Live joyfully with the wife whom thou lovest all the days of the life of thy vanity, which he hath given thee under the sun, all the days of thy vanity: for that is thy portion in this life, and in thy labour which thou takest under the sun. Whatsoever thy hand findeth to do, do it with thy might; for there is no work, nor device, nor knowledge, nor wisdom, in the grave, whither thou goest. I returned, and saw under the sun, that the race is not to the swift, nor the battle to the strong, neither yet bread to the wise, nor yet riches to men of understanding, nor yet favour to men of skill; but time and chance happeneth to them all.

Ecclesiastes 9:4-11

2258. You are the *gift*. Keep being your best daily. Keep on loving your children and family. Keep being diligent in your service to the people on your job. Keep being kind to strangers in the grocery store and drive-thru. Keep being a contender in the game of life. You are the gift. Keep on loving, living, and giving of your worth into life. You will continue to accumulate in value over time like *compound interest*.

He that diligently seeketh good procureth favour: but he that seeketh mischief, it shall come unto him.

> Proverbs 11:27

2259. Happy New Year! Freedom in the spirit is yours this year. The Spirit flows with your heart's desires this year. All favor flows in your direction this year. Breathe! You are free to flow in the prosperity of God in all that you set your hands to this year! Health flows to you this year! Victory over all opposition is yours this year. Choose life. God has allowed a spiritual release for your family, health, prosperity, and good name. Happy New Year to you and yours! In Jesus name, amen.

And thus shall ye say to him that liveth in prosperity, peace be both to thee, and peace be to thine house, and peace be unto all that thou hast.

> 1 Samuel 25:6

2260. It takes a successful person to truly recognize a success. People who have never tried or succeeded couldn't really recognize a success while it's happening. It takes a success to recognize a success.

He that is despised, and hath a servant, is better than he that honoureth himself, and lacketh bread.

> Proverbs 12:9

2261. Never try to fit the vision of a big thinker into the mind of a limited thinker. The vision will surely suffer a contorted reduction, and if, by chance, there's an attempt to execute the vision, the results will certainly be less than at first visualized. The achievement of big visions requires big thinking. Big thinking requires you to stretch to let go of limited thinking.

And the disciples of John and of the Pharisees used to fast: and they come and say unto him, why do the disciples of John and of the Pharisees fast, but thy disciples fast not? And Jesus said unto them, can the children of the bridechamber fast, while the bridegroom is with them? As long as they have the bridegroom with them, they cannot fast. But the days will come, when the bridegroom shall be taken away from them, and then shall they fast in those days. No man also seweth a piece of new cloth on an old garment: else the new piece that filled it up taketh away from the old, and the rent is made worse. And no man putteth new wine into old bottles: else the new wine doth burst the bottles, and the wine is spilled, and the bottles will be marred: but new wine must be put into new bottles.

Mark 2:18-22

2262. Regarding people's behavior, one or two times, it may be a mistake. Three or four times, it's a habit. *All of the time*, it's the nature.

Even a child is known by his doings, whether his work be pure, and whether it be right.

>   Proverbs 20:11

2263. Just like the wife was a wife before she was married, the king was the king before he was *crowned*. A virtuous woman is a crown to her husband. She's proof that he was already a king.

A virtuous woman is a crown to her husband: but she that maketh ashamed is as rottenness in his bones.

>   Proverbs 12:4

2264. Regarding dreams, it never pays to listen to naysayers. It always ultimately pays to listen to your dream.

Now therefore be not grieved, nor angry with yourselves, that ye sold me hither: for God did send me before you to preserve life. For these two years hath the famine been in the land: and yet there are five years, in the which there shall neither be earing nor harvest. And God sent me before you to preserve you a posterity in the earth, and to save your lives by a great deliverance. So now it was not you that sent me hither, but God: and he hath made me a father to Pharaoh, and Lord of all his house, and a ruler throughout all the land of Egypt. Haste ye, and go up to my father, and say unto him, thus saith thy son Joseph, God hath made me Lord of all Egypt: come down unto me, tarry not: and thou shalt dwell in the land of Goshen, and thou shalt be near unto me, thou, and thy children, and thy children's children, and thy flocks, and thy herds, and all that thou hast: and there will I nourish thee; for yet there are

five years of famine; lest thou, and thy household, and all that thou hast, come to poverty.

Genesis 45:5-11

2265. If you refuse to be manipulated anymore, then, you quickly cure manipulators. That's the most gracious thing that you can do for them.

And it came to pass, as we went to prayer, a certain damsel possessed with a spirit of divination met us, which brought her masters much gain by soothsaying: The same followed Paul and us, and cried, saying, these men are the servants of the most high God, which shew unto us the way of salvation. And this did she many days. But Paul, being grieved, turned and said to the spirit, I command thee in the name of Jesus Christ to come out of her. And he came out the same hour.

Acts 16:16-18

2266. If you want wealth and longevity, you must live like a king, but eat like a pauper. Eat beans, greens, vegetables, fruit, fish, spare meats, etc., in the most luxurious settings. Live like a king. Eat like a pauper. When you become a *"fat-cat"* in wealth, you can't eat like a *"fat-cat"*, or you will end up a *dead cat*! If you want wealth and longevity, you must live like a king, but eat like a pauper.

Prove thy servants, I beseech thee, ten days; and let them give us pulse to eat, and water to drink. Then let our countenances be looked upon before thee, and the countenance of the

children that eat of the portion of the king's meat: and as thou seest, deal with thy servants. So he consented to them in this matter, and proved them ten days. And at the end of ten days their countenances appeared fairer and fatter in flesh than all the children which did eat the portion of the king's meat. Thus Melzar took away the portion of their meat, and the wine that they should drink; and gave them pulse. As for these four children, God gave them knowledge and skill in all learning and wisdom: and Daniel had understanding in all visions and dreams. Now at the end of the days that the king had said he should bring them in, then the prince of the eunuchs brought them in before Nebuchadnezzar. And the king communed with them; and among them all was found none like Daniel, Hananiah, Mishael, and Azariah: therefore stood they before the king. And in all matters of wisdom and understanding, that the king enquired of them, he found them ten times better than all the magicians and astrologers that were in all his realm. And Daniel continued even unto the first year of king Cyrus.

Daniel 1:12-21

2267. Righteousness always prevails over wickedness. Righteous power always prevails over wicked power. Specifically, when the righteous power stands and exercises their authority.

Behold, I give unto you power to tread on serpents and scorpions, and over all the power of the enemy: and nothing shall by any means hurt you. Notwithstanding in this rejoice

not, that the spirits are subject unto you; but rather rejoice, because your names are written in heaven.

Luke 10:19-20

2268. Regarding intentions, if it's not straightforward, then, it's not God. God is straightforward regarding His intentions for us.

Who is a wise man and endued with knowledge among you? Let him shew out of a good conversation his works with meekness of wisdom. But if ye have bitter envying and strife in your hearts, glory not, and lie not against the truth. This wisdom descendeth not from above, but is earthly, sensual, devilish. For where envying and strife is, there is confusion and every evil work. But the wisdom that is from above is first pure, then peaceable, gentle, and easy to be intreated, full of mercy and good fruits, without partiality, and without hypocrisy. And the fruit of righteousness is sown in peace of them that make peace.

James 3:13-18

2269. A marriage is what you make it. If a man and woman want to make it, then, they'll make it.

And he answered and said unto them, have ye not read, that he which made them at the beginning made them male and female, and said, for this cause shall a man leave father and mother, and shall cleave to his wife: and they twain shall be one flesh? Wherefore they are no more twain, but one flesh.

What therefore God hath joined together, let not man put asunder.

> Matthew 19:4-6

2270. It's unapologetically winter.

Hast thou entered into the treasures of the snow? Or hast thou seen the treasures of the hail, which I have reserved against the time of trouble, against the day of battle and war?

> Job 38:22-23

2271. You should value your thoughts enough to record them.

The thoughts of the diligent tend only to plenteousness...

> Proverbs 21:5a

2272. Shoot for the highest reward in pay. Don't let anyone talk you out of your highest potential. Don't be afraid of challenges. Challenges make champions. Challenges are how you get ahead in life.

And the men of Israel said, have ye seen this man that is come up? Surely to defy Israel is he come up: and it shall be, that the man who killeth him, the king will enrich him with great riches, and will give him his daughter, and make his father's house free in Israel. And David spake to the men that stood by him, saying, what shall be done to the man that killeth this Philistine, and taketh away the reproach from Israel? For who

is this uncircumcised Philistine, that he should defy the armies of the living God? And the people answered him after this manner, saying, so shall it be done to the man that killeth him. And Eliab his eldest brother heard when he spake unto the men; and Eliab's anger was kindled against David, and he said, why camest thou down hither? And with whom hast thou left those few sheep in the wilderness? I know thy pride, and the naughtiness of thine heart; for thou art come down that thou mightest see the battle. And David said, what have I now done? Is there not a cause? And he turned from him toward another, and spake after the same manner: and the people answered him again after the former manner. And when the words were heard which David spake, they rehearsed them before Saul: and he sent for him. And David said to Saul, let no man's heart fail because of him; thy servant will go and fight with this Philistine.

1 Samuel 17:25-32

2273. Evaluate your life like a long-term investor. Don't be so moved by the spikes and drops, or the ups and downs. Rather, be moved by the trends. Invest your energy, money, and time based on the trends in regard to people, places, events, and opportunities.

Cast thy bread upon the waters: for thou shalt find it after many days. Give a portion to seven, and also to eight; for thou knowest not what evil shall be upon the earth. If the clouds be full of rain, they empty themselves upon the earth: and if the tree fall toward the south, or toward the north, in the place where the tree falleth, there it shall be. He that observeth the

wind shall not sow; and he that regardeth the clouds shall not reap. As thou knowest not what is the way of the spirit, nor how the bones do grow in the womb of her that is with child: even so thou knowest not the works of God who maketh all. In the morning sow thy seed, and in the evening withhold not thine hand: for thou knowest not whether shall prosper, either this or that, or whether they both shall be alike good.

Ecclesiastes 11:1-6

2274. The time to confess is when you've done something that God can bless!

A man shall be satisfied with good by the fruit of his mouth: and the recompence of a man's hands shall be rendered unto him.

Proverbs 12:14

2275. Regarding sales, the key to promotion is *promotion*.

That the communication of thy faith may become effectual by the acknowledging of every good thing which is in you in Christ Jesus.

Philemon 1:6

2276. Condemnation, guilt, shaming, blaming, and criticism are not God's ways. Those are the ways of the devil. Those who operate in these methods as a means of controlling people and situations, are not operating in the ways of God.

They are operating in fleshy wisdom. God exposes sin. God forgives sin. God judges sin. God gives grace to change. That's the way of God.

The Lord hath appeared of old unto me, saying, yea, I have loved thee with an everlasting love: therefore with lovingkindness have I drawn thee.

> Jeremiah 31:3

2277. In regard to destiny and strength, you have the strength for where you are, but you're going to have the strength for where you're going.

Thy shoes shall be iron and brass; and as thy days, so shall thy strength be.

> Deuteronomy 33:25

2278. A bird that doesn't sing doesn't give God any glory!

It is a good thing to give thanks unto the Lord, and to sing praises unto thy name, O most high: to shew forth thy lovingkindness in the morning, and thy faithfulness every night.

> Psalm 92:1-2

2279. When you're traveling on God's path and you can't see the next turn, then, don't worry, because God can. He will open up a door in the middle of the road for you.

I know thy works: behold, I have set before thee an open door, and no man can shut it: for thou hast a little strength, and hast kept my word, and hast not denied my name.

Revelation 3:8

2280. Regarding how to avoid headaches in life, always think problem prevention, because, if it could happen . . . it could happen.

A prudent man foreseeth the evil, and hideth himself; but the simple pass on, and are punished.

Proverbs 27:12

2281. One generation believes in veiled communication and insinuation, whereas, another generation believes in *"keeping it real."*

Now Elihu had waited till Job had spoken, because they were elder than he. When Elihu saw that there was no answer in the mouth of these three men, then his wrath was kindled. And Elihu the son of Barachel the Buzite answered and said, I am young, and ye are very old; wherefore I was afraid, and durst not shew you mine opinion. I said, days should speak, and multitude of years should teach wisdom. But there is a spirit in man: and the inspiration of the almighty giveth them understanding. Great men are not always wise: neither do the aged understand judgment. Therefore I said, hearken to me; I also will shew mine opinion. Behold, I waited for your words; I gave ear to your reasons, whilst ye searched out what to say.

Pastor Terrance Levise Turner, MBA

Yea, I attended unto you, and, behold, there was none of you that convinced Job, or that answered his words: lest ye should say, we have found out wisdom: God thrusteth him down, not man. Now he hath not directed his words against me: neither will I answer him with your speeches. They were amazed, they answered no more: they left off speaking. When I had waited, (for they spake not, but stood still, and answered no more;) I said, I will answer also my part, I also will shew mine opinion. For I am full of matter, the spirit within me constraineth me. Behold, my belly is as wine which hath no vent; it is ready to burst like new bottles. I will speak, that I may be refreshed: I will open my lips and answer. Let me not, I pray you, accept any man's person, neither let me give flattering titles unto man. For I know not to give flattering titles; in so doing my maker would soon take me away.

Job 32:4-22

2282. Inspiration without information leads to frustration. The rightly divided Word of God is the key to financial deliverance. It takes more than an emotional catharsis to become free. The Spirit of the Lord is upon His preachers, and He has anointed them to bring deliverance to His people. However, inspiration without information leads to frustration. Wisdom is the principal thing that leads to freedom. Knowledge and understanding is the key to success.

And I will give you pastors according to mine heart, which shall feed you with knowledge and understanding. And it shall come to pass, when ye be multiplied and increased in the land, in those days, saith the Lord, they shall say no more, the ark of

the covenant of the Lord: neither shall it come to mind: neither shall they remember it; neither shall they visit it; neither shall that be done any more. At that time they shall call Jerusalem the throne of the Lord; and all the nations shall be gathered unto it, to the name of the Lord, to Jerusalem: neither shall they walk any more after the imagination of their evil heart.

Jeremiah 3:15-17

2283. Regarding marketing and sales and promotions, choose publicity over profit, and you'll eventually have profit.

But rather seek ye the kingdom of God; and all these things shall be added unto you. Fear not, little flock; for it is your father's good pleasure to give you the kingdom. Sell that ye have, and give alms; provide yourselves bags which wax not old, a treasure in the heavens that faileth not, where no thief approacheth, neither moth corrupteth. For where your treasure is, there will your heart be also.

Luke 12:31-34

2284. Regarding finding your purpose, life is like shopping at the grocery store. When you know what you really want, it doesn't take as long.

Trust in the Lord, and do good; so shalt thou dwell in the land, and verily thou shalt be fed. Delight thyself also in the Lord: and he shall give thee the desires of thine heart. Commit thy way unto the Lord; trust also in him; and he shall bring it to

pass. And he shall bring forth thy righteousness as the light, and thy judgment as the noonday.

> Psalm 37:3-6

2285. Any deal entered into that wasn't freely and mutually negotiated to equally benefit the two parties ends in extortion.

It is naught, it is naught, saith the buyer: but when he is gone his way, then he boasteth.

> Proverbs 20:14

2286. Regarding the road to destiny, don't wait until the battle is over. Rather, shout now! Rejoice now! Be proud of your process! Be happy in the moment! Be thankful for the journey. Don't wait until the battle is over. Shout now!

And it was told king David, saying, the Lord hath blessed the house of Obededom, and all that pertaineth unto him, because of the ark of God. So David went and brought up the ark of God from the house of Obededom into the city of David with gladness. And it was so, that when they that bare the ark of the Lord had gone six paces, he sacrificed oxen and fatlings. And David danced before the Lord with all his might; and David was girded with a linen ephod. So David and all the house of Israel brought up the ark of the Lord with shouting, and with the sound of the trumpet.

> 2 Samuel 6:12-15

2287. In regard to being a chosen vessel of God, when envied by others, tell your enemies "It's not a matter of who *I* think I am. Rather, it's a matter of who God *knows* I am. If God be for me, who can be against me!"

And the patriarchs, moved with envy, sold Joseph into Egypt: but God was with him, And delivered him out of all his afflictions, and gave him favour and wisdom in the sight of pharaoh king of Egypt; and he made him governor over Egypt and all his house.

Acts 7:9-10

2288. Regarding tests, the test is not for you to *fail* the test. The test is for you to be *prepared* for the test. It forces you to *study* for the test.

Study to shew thyself approved unto God, a workman that needeth not to be ashamed, rightly dividing the word of truth.

2 Timothy 2:15

2289. You're living in legendary times. So, make a show! Make the most of your moment. This is your time to write a page in history.

So teach us to number our days, that we may apply our hearts unto wisdom.

Psalm 90:12

2290. Everything starts with a seed. You often ask God for a *thing*. However, God usually doesn't give you the *thing*. He gives you the *seed* for the thing. He doesn't give you the career or business. He gives you the *desire* for the career or business. The desire is the seed for the actual thing. God then gives you stewardship of the seed. Your extent of commitment will determine if you will get the *thing*.

The sower soweth the word. And these are they by the way side, where the word is sown; but when they have heard, Satan cometh immediately, and taketh away the word that was sown in their hearts. And these are they likewise which are sown on stony ground; who, when they have heard the word, immediately receive it with gladness; and have no root in themselves, and so endure but for a time: afterward, when affliction or persecution ariseth for the word's sake, immediately they are offended. And these are they which are sown among thorns; such as hear the word, and the cares of this world, and the deceitfulness of riches, and the lusts of other things entering in, choke the word, and it becometh unfruitful. And these are they which are sown on good ground; such as hear the word, and receive it, and bring forth fruit, some thirtyfold, some sixty, and some an hundred.

Mark 4:14-20

2291. There are various kinds and applications of faith for various things that you need. There's faith for healing. There's faith for buying houses, businesses, and properties. There's faith for selling goods, products, and services. There's faith for

producing books, music projects, and movies. There's faith for various applications, and there's various sources for that faith. Let God's Word and principles be the foundation for your faith. However, also listen to those who have successfully used His principles in various applications.

And they rose early in the morning, and went forth into the wilderness of Tekoa: and as they went forth, Jehoshaphat stood and said, hear me, O Judah, and ye inhabitants of Jerusalem; believe in the Lord your God, so shall ye be established; believe his prophets, so shall ye prosper.

2 Chronicles 20:20

2292. In regard to the journey of faith, keep holding on. Keep getting up. Keep going forward.

The righteous also shall hold on his way, and he that hath clean hands shall be stronger and stronger.

Job 17:9

2293. Eagles don't flap . . .they soar! Eagles are dignified in how they do their thing. They have long-distance vision. They see more of the sky. Therefore, they don't have to be nervous about the obscurity of cloudy conditions. They just mount up and soar like the eagles they are.

But they that wait upon the Lord shall renew their strength; they shall mount up with wings as eagles; they shall run, and not be weary; and they shall walk, and not faint.

Isaiah 40:31

2294. Making a wage is automatic. Making a profit takes planning. To make a wage, you must get a job. To make a profit, you must run a successful business. Making a wage will pay the bills. Moreover, consistently making a profit will *set you free.*

And that ye study to be quiet, and to do your own business, and to work with your own hands, as we commanded you; that ye may walk honestly toward them that are without, and that ye may have lack of nothing.

1 Thessalonians 4:11-12

2295. Regarding vision, seeing is believing, and then, believing is achieving. If you can see it on the inside, you can achieve it on the outside!

Where there is no vision, the people perish: but he that keepeth the law, happy is he.

Proverbs 29:18

2296. As you focus on increasing in value, you automatically eventually will increase in compensation. As you also increase in marketing your value, you will obtain that compensation.

In the morning sow thy seed, and in the evening withhold not thine hand: for thou knowest not whether shall prosper, either this or that, or whether they both shall be alike good.

Ecclesiastes 11:6

2297. Regarding advice for success, don't listen to *zeros*, when you know you're *100%*.

He that is despised, and hath a servant, is better than he that honoureth himself, and lacketh bread.

Proverbs 12:9

2298. In a fraction, the denominator is the number below the line. It's the number of equal parts into which a whole number can be divided. In other words, the denominator breaks things down to the *bottom line*. It helps you get things down to the basics so that you can understand and work with it better. So, I guess it's not too bad to be a *denominator*.

Study to shew thyself approved unto God, a workman that needeth not to be ashamed, rightly dividing the word of truth.

2 Timothy 2:15

2299. You cannot tell a builder that he or she doesn't have a house, if he or she has a blueprint, time, energy, and materials. He or she does have a house. When he or she has the blueprint, all that he or she has to do is to initiate and carry

out the plan. You can't tell a builder that he or she doesn't have a house, if he or she has a blueprint.

And they said, go to, let us build us a city and a tower, whose top may reach unto heaven; and let us make us a name, lest we be scattered abroad upon the face of the whole earth. And the Lord came down to see the city and the tower, which the children of men builded. And the Lord said, behold, the people is one, and they have all one language; and this they begin to do: and now nothing will be restrained from them, which they have imagined to do.

Genesis 11:4-6

2300. Now, more than ever, it's of critical importance that Christians pray in the Holy Ghost. It's not just a suggestion. It's not optional. It's a vital survival tool for walking in the spirit in the world in which we live.

But ye, beloved, building up yourselves on your most holy faith, praying in the Holy Ghost, keep yourselves in the love of God, looking for the mercy of our Lord Jesus Christ unto eternal life.

Jude 20-21

2301. In regard to your children, you must handle them with care. You are raising a deliver.

And there was a certain man of Zorah, of the family of the Danites, whose name was Manoah; and his wife was barren,

and bare not. And the angel of the Lord appeared unto the woman, and said unto her, behold now, thou art barren, and bearest not: but thou shalt conceive, and bear a son. Now therefore beware, I pray thee, and drink not wine nor strong drink, and eat not any unclean thing: for, lo, thou shalt conceive, and bear a son; and no razor shall come on his head: for the child shall be a Nazarite unto God from the womb: and he shall begin to deliver Israel out of the hand of the Philistines. Then the woman came and told her husband, saying, a man of God came unto me, and his countenance was like the countenance of an angel of God, very terrible: but I asked him not whence he was, neither told he me his name: but he said unto me, behold, thou shalt conceive, and bear a son; and now drink no wine nor strong drink, neither eat any unclean thing: for the child shall be a Nazarite to God from the womb to the day of his death. Then Manoah intreated the Lord, and said, O my Lord, let the man of God which thou didst send come again unto us, and teach us what we shall do unto the child that shall be born. And God hearkened to the voice of Manoah; and the angel of God came again unto the woman as she sat in the field: but Manoah her husband was not with her. And the woman made haste, and ran, and shewed her husband, and said unto him, behold, the man hath appeared unto me, that came unto me the other day. And Manoah arose, and went after his wife, and came to the man, and said unto him, art thou the man that spakest unto the woman? And he said, I am. And Manoah said, now let thy words come to pass. How shall we order the child, and how shall we do unto him? And the angel of the Lord said unto Manoah, of all that I said unto the woman let her beware.

Judges 13:2-13

2302. I pray that the blessing of God will continue to rest upon you and all of your endeavors. May God protect and surround you and your family with His angelic hosts. May your faith be strengthened day by day, and may you have peace. In Jesus name, amen.

The Lord bless thee, and keep thee: the Lord make his face shine upon thee, and be gracious unto thee: the Lord lift up his countenance upon thee, and give thee peace.

Numbers 6:24-26

2303. People who are "in the know", because they are "*in the do*" are the people to listen to, because they are the people who truly *know*. They've "*been there, done that, and have gotten the t-shirt*". They are the ones who can advise you about getting your *t-shirt*. They are less likely to be jealous of the size of your t-shirt. They are still in the struggle with you. The people who are "in the know", because they are "in the do" are the ones you should listen to.

That ye be not slothful, but followers of them who through faith and patience inherit the promises.

Hebrews 6:12

2304. *Thinking people* ask questions. *Unthinking people* are afraid to ask questions. God is gracious and all wise. He can handle your questions.

Distinguished Wisdom Presents... "Living Proverbs"–Vol.5

If any of you lack wisdom, let him ask of God, that giveth to all men liberally, and upbraideth not; and it shall be given him.

James 1:5

2305. You can't avoid life. You can't run from life, because, eventually, life will catch up with you. You have to *run at life*! Take on your giants!

And he took his staff in his hand, and chose him five smooth stones out of the brook, and put them in a shepherd's bag which he had, even in a scrip; and his sling was in his hand: and he drew near to the Philistine. And the Philistine came on and drew near unto David; and the man that bare the shield went before him. And when the Philistine looked about, and saw David, he disdained him: for he was but a youth, and ruddy, and of a fair countenance. And the Philistine said unto David, am I a dog, that thou comest to me with staves? And the Philistine cursed David by his gods. And the Philistine said to David, come to me, and I will give thy flesh unto the fowls of the air, and to the beasts of the field. Then said David to the Philistine, thou comest to me with a sword, and with a spear, and with a shield: but I come to thee in the name of the Lord of hosts, the God of the armies of Israel, whom thou hast defied. This day will the Lord deliver thee into mine hand; and I will smite thee, and take thine head from thee; and I will give the carcases of the host of the Philistines this day unto the fowls of the air, and to the wild beasts of the earth; that all the earth may know that there is a God in Israel. And all this assembly shall know that the Lord saveth not with sword and spear: for the battle is the Lord's, and he will give you into our

hands. And it came to pass, when the Philistine arose, and came, and drew nigh to meet David, that David hastened, and ran toward the army to meet the Philistine. And David put his hand in his bag, and took thence a stone, and slang it, and smote the Philistine in his forehead, that the stone sunk into his forehead; and he fell upon his face to the earth. So David prevailed over the Philistine with a sling and with a stone, and smote the Philistine, and slew him; but there was no sword in the hand of David. Therefore David ran, and stood upon the Philistine, and took his sword, and drew it out of the sheath thereof, and slew him, and cut off his head therewith. And when the Philistines saw their champion was dead, they fled.

1 Samuel 17:40-51

2306. Only people of purpose can truly understand the *woes and perils* of progress. The uninitiated, innocent bystanders can only comment upon what they are too afraid to venture out into. Only people of purpose will eventually be successful, satisfied, and vindicated by the *sweet taste of victory*!

But none of these things move me, neither count I my life dear unto myself, so that I might finish my course with joy, and the ministry, which I have received of the Lord Jesus, to testify the gospel of the grace of God.

Acts 20:24

2307. You are a rich person if you can get a prayer through to Heaven. Being able to get a prayer through to Heaven will get you out of the pit, and will keep you out of the grave.

Whether you're black, white, old, young, rich, poor, fat, or skinny, being able to get a prayer through to God will get you out of the pit. Prayer will keep you in life. If you can get a prayer through, then, you are a rich person!

Confess your faults one to another, and pray one for another, that ye may be healed. The effectual fervent prayer of a righteous man availeth much. Elias was a man subject to like passions as we are, and he prayed earnestly that it might not rain: and it rained not on the earth by the space of three years and six months. And he prayed again, and the heaven gave rain, and the earth brought forth her fruit.

James 5:16-18

2308. Regarding abundance and scarcity, it's always better to have more than less. God is the God of abundance. He wishes above all things that you prosper, and be in health, even as your souls prosper.

Beloved, I wish above all things that thou mayest prosper and be in health, even as thy soul prospereth.

3 John 2

2309. All of work doesn't require using a pick and a shovel to dig a ditch. Some work requires a sound, creative mind, and the willingness to use it to prosper.

And that ye study to be quiet, and to do your own business, and to work with your own hands, as we commanded you;

that ye may walk honestly toward them that are without, and that ye may have lack of nothing.

1 Thessalonians 4:11-12

2310. Your ability to say *no* empowers you to say *yes*.

The heart of the righteous studieth to answer: but the mouth of the wicked poureth out evil things.

Proverbs 15:28

2311. It doesn't take a lot to do what's right. It just takes a will to do what's right.

To do justice and judgment is more acceptable to the Lord than sacrifice.

Proverbs 21:3

2312. Education is not required for intelligence. There are a lot of Mamas and Papas, Grandmamas and Granddaddys that are "Here by being careful!" They've been able to navigate through life in spite of their lack of education or opportunity. They have God-given wisdom that has helped them to raise up the next generation. Education is not required for intelligence.

And there went a man of the house of Levi, and took to wife a daughter of Levi.

And the woman conceived, and bare a son: and when she saw him that he was a goodly child, she hid him three months. And when she could not longer hide him, she took for him an ark of bulrushes, and daubed it with slime and with pitch, and put the child therein; and she laid it in the flags by the river's brink. And his sister stood afar off, to wit what would be done to him. And the daughter of pharaoh came down to wash herself at the river; and her maidens walked along by the river's side; and when she saw the ark among the flags, she sent her maid to fetch it. And when she had opened it, she saw the child: and, behold, the babe wept. And she had compassion on him, and said, this is one of the Hebrews' children. Then said his sister to pharaoh's daughter, shall I go and call to thee a nurse of the Hebrew women, that she may nurse the child for thee? And pharaoh's daughter said to her, go. And the maid went and called the child's mother. And pharaoh's daughter said unto her, take this child away, and nurse it for me, and I will give thee thy wages. And the women took the child, and nursed it. And the child grew, and she brought him unto pharaoh's daughter, and he became her son. And she called his name Moses: and she said, because I drew him out of the water.

Exodus 2:1-10

2313. Rather than believing for a causeless miracle, believe God for an exceptional fulfillment of His promised principles. Work the principle in faith, and then, you will have cause to believe for miraculous results. God will put His *"super"* on your natural, and you will get a *supernatural* result. He will put

His "extra" on your ordinary, and you will get an *extraordinary* outcome.

But whoso looketh into the perfect law of liberty, and continueth therein, he being not a forgetful hearer, but a doer of the work, this man shall be blessed in his deed.

James 1:25

2314. In regard to sin in our society, listen to the voices of outcry, or the lack thereof, to measure the level of morality in our society. Society may change in its evaluation of sin, but God doesn't. Repentance is the only remedy for sin, according to God's Word.

Fools make a mock at sin: but among the righteous there is favour.

Proverbs 14:9

2315. If you've been sailing along in what seems to be a mist or fog, and it seems that you've suddenly run upon the rocks of life...don't be discouraged! Look up! You may have actually run into an unseen *lighthouse*. Many times, in the darkest moments of bewilderment is when we discover the *light of life* that will lead us into our destined port of prosperity and blessing. Be encouraged and keep sailing forward!

For our light affliction, which is but for a moment, worketh for us a far more exceeding and eternal weight of glory.

2 Corinthians 4:17

2316. Enter into the faith-zone. When you enter into the faith-zone, you will enter into the *favor-zone*. Faith procures favor.

He that diligently seeketh good procureth favour: but he that seeketh mischief, it shall come unto him.

Proverbs 11:27

2317. We walk by faith and not by sight. Really, that's the only and best way to walk. We don't control everything. However, we can walk knowing the One Who does. Therefore, we can have joy on the journey, while walking by faith and not by sight.

The earth is the Lord's, and the fulness thereof; the world, and they that dwell therein.

Psalm 24:1

2318. Based on the evidence, you have a very good chance of living close to 120 years of age. In 2017, the oldest person in the world was a Jamaican woman named Mrs. Violet Moss Brown. She died at 117 years old. You have so much better healthcare and lifestyle opportunities than she ever imagined. If we all would only change our perspective and paradigm regarding life expectancy, then, it's very reasonable that we would live much longer.

And the Lord said, my spirit shall not always strive with man, for that he also is flesh: yet his days shall be an hundred and twenty years.

> Genesis 6:3

2319. One of the best ways to be successful is to read autobiographies of successful people. Then say, "If they could do it, I will too!" Then, get busy studying how. Then, do what they did. Success is available to all!

And that ye study to be quiet, and to do your own business, and to work with your own hands, as we commanded you; that ye may walk honestly toward them that are without, and that ye may have lack of nothing.

> 1 Thessalonians 4:11-12

2320. If loving me is wrong, I don't want to be right. If being me is wrong, I don't want to be right. True love begins with loving yourself.

I will praise thee; for I am fearfully and wonderfully made: marvellous are thy works; and that my soul knoweth right well. My substance was not hid from thee, when I was made in secret, and curiously wrought in the lowest parts of the earth. Thine eyes did see my substance, yet being unperfect; and in thy book all my members were written, which in continuance were fashioned, when as yet there was none of them. How precious also are thy thoughts unto me, O God! How great is

the sum of them! If I should count them, they are more in number than the sand: when I awake, I am still with thee.

Psalm 139:14-18

2321. Don't be envious. Trust God, and get busy. Do what's necessary to change your situation. You won't have to be envious of others.

Then Peter opened his mouth, and said, of a truth I perceive that God is no respecter of persons: but in every nation he that feareth him, and worketh righteousness, is accepted with him.

Acts 10:34-35

2322. Always hear with a discerning ear. From words dreams rise or disappear. Listen for faith. Avoid words of fear. The words you discern will determine what will appear. Always hear with a discerning ear.

So then faith cometh by hearing, and hearing by the word of God.

Romans 10:17

2323. Certain behaviors, events, decisions, and judgments in society impact or license themselves to be repeated, perpetuated, and overlooked based on how the high profile initial event was handled. God will judge judges. God will

Pastor Terrance Levise Turner, MBA

discipline His decision-makers based on how they behave and judge in society.

Now it came to pass in the days of Ahasuerus, (this is Ahasuerus which reigned, from India even unto Ethiopia, over an hundred and seven and twenty provinces:) That in those days, when the king Ahasuerus sat on the throne of his kingdom, which was in Shushan the palace, in the third year of his reign, he made a feast unto all his princes and his servants; the power of Persia and Media, the nobles and princes of the provinces, being before him: when he shewed the riches of his glorious kingdom and the honour of his excellent majesty many days, even an hundred and fourscore days. And when these days were expired, the king made a feast unto all the people that were present in Shushan the palace, both unto great and small, seven days, in the court of the garden of the king's palace; where were white, green, and blue, hangings, fastened with cords of fine linen and purple to silver rings and pillars of marble: the beds were of gold and silver, upon a pavement of red, and blue, and white, and black, marble. And they gave them drink in vessels of gold, (the vessels being diverse one from another,) and royal wine in abundance, according to the state of the king. And the drinking was according to the law; none did compel: for so the king had appointed to all the officers of his house, that they should do according to every man's pleasure. Also Vashti the queen made a feast for the women in the royal house which belonged to king Ahasuerus. On the seventh day, when the heart of the king was merry with wine, he commanded Mehuman, Biztha, Harbona, Bigtha, and Abagtha, Zethar, and Carcas, the seven chamberlains that served in the presence of

Ahasuerus the king, to bring Vashti the queen before the king with the crown royal, to shew the people and the princes her beauty: for she was fair to look on. But the queen Vashti refused to come at the king's commandment by his chamberlains: therefore was the king very wroth, and his anger burned in him. Then the king said to the wise men, which knew the times, (for so was the king's manner toward all that knew law and judgment: and the next unto him was Carshena, Shethar, Admatha, Tarshish, Meres, Marsena, and Memucan, the seven princes of Persia and Media, which saw the king's face, and which sat the first in the kingdom;) what shall we do unto the queen Vashti according to law, because she hath not performed the commandment of the king Ahasuerus by the chamberlains? And Memucan answered before the king and the princes, Vashti the queen hath not done wrong to the king only, but also to all the princes, and to all the people that are in all the provinces of the king Ahasuerus. For this deed of the queen shall come abroad unto all women, so that they shall despise their husbands in their eyes, when it shall be reported, the king Ahasuerus commanded Vashti the queen to be brought in before him, but she came not. Likewise shall the ladies of Persia and Media say this day unto all the king's princes, which have heard of the deed of the queen. Thus shall there arise too much contempt and wrath. If it please the king, let there go a royal commandment from him, and let it be written among the laws of the Persians and the Medes, that it be not altered, that Vashti come no more before king Ahasuerus; and let the king give her royal estate unto another that is better than she. And when the king's decree which he shall make shall be published throughout all his empire, (for it is great,) all the wives shall

give to their husbands honour, both to great and small. And the saying pleased the king and the princes; and the king did according to the word of Memucan: for he sent letters into all the king's provinces, into every province according to the writing thereof, and to every people after their language, that every man should bear rule in his own house, and that it should be published according to the language of every people.

Esther 1

2324. You don't have to bow and cater to the favor of another to be blessed in society. You don't have to serve the opinion of another in order to be free in society. You were *born* free. You were born with God-given rights. You were made in the image and likeness of God Himself.

And I will walk at liberty: for I seek thy precepts. I will speak of thy testimonies also before kings, and will not be ashamed.

Psalm 119:45-46

2325. A lot of times we ask God "What do I do? What do I do?" And, often He doesn't tell us what to do, but He gives us the courage to do what we know we ought to do.

There hath no temptation taken you but such as is common to man: but God is faithful, who will not suffer you to be tempted above that ye are able; but will with the temptation also make a way to escape, that ye may be able to bear it.

1 Corinthians 10:13

2326. You are a success going somewhere to happen!

I can do all things through Christ, which strengtheneth me.

Philippians 4:13

2327. You are not who others say you are. You are who *you* say you are. If you agree with who God's says you are, then, you will be all that you are supposed to be. Always agree with God.

That the communication of thy faith may become effectual by the acknowledging of every good thing, which is in you in Christ Jesus.

Philemon 1:6

2328. You are a kingpin. You are a *hinge-pin* upon which the door to the future swings! Fulfill your service to mankind, and new opportunities will be ushered into the earth!

For if thou altogether holdest thy peace at this time, then shall there enlargement and deliverance arise to the Jews from another place; but thou and thy father's house shall be destroyed: and who knoweth whether thou art come to the kingdom for such a time as this?

Esther 4:14

2329. Regarding doing right, you don't need a spotlight. Just do what you know is right, whether day or night, and God will reward you with favor when the time is right, because you are seen in your Heavenly Father's sight.

Therefore when thou doest thine alms, do not sound a trumpet before thee, as the hypocrites do in the synagogues and in the streets, that they may have glory of men. Verily I say unto you, they have their reward. But when thou doest alms, let not thy left hand know what thy right hand doeth: that thine alms may be in secret: and thy father which seeth in secret himself shall reward thee openly. And when thou prayest, thou shalt not be as the hypocrites are: for they love to pray standing in the synagogues and in the corners of the streets, that they may be seen of men. Verily I say unto you, they have their reward. But thou, when thou prayest, enter into thy closet, and when thou hast shut thy door, pray to thy father which is in secret; and thy father which seeth in secret shall reward thee openly.

Matthew 6:2-6

2330. Only tolerate noble deeds and noble thoughts. Surround yourself with uplifting spirits. Surround yourself with those who aspire to greatness, and who have conversation and deeds to match. Disassociate yourself from ignoble personalities, whose thoughts and words weaken your sense of nobility.

These were more noble than those in Thessalonica, in that they received the word with all readiness of mind, and

searched the scriptures daily, whether those things were so. Therefore many of them believed; also of honourable women which were Greeks, and of men, not a few.

Acts 17:11-12

2331. Your faith may not always be accompanied by feelings. You may have questions with your faith. It's ok. You have been trained in righteousness. Therefore, carryout the righteousness you have been trained to do. There are promises attached to that righteousness. There are rewards attached to righteousness. Fulfill all righteousness, and leave the questions and answers to God.

Then cometh Jesus from Galilee to Jordan unto John, to be baptized of him. But John forbad him, saying, I have need to be baptized of thee, and comest thou to me? And Jesus answering said unto him, suffer it to be so now: for thus it becometh us to fulfil all righteousness. Then he suffered him. And Jesus, when he was baptized, went up straightway out of the water: and, lo, the heavens were opened unto him, and he saw the spirit of God descending like a dove, and lighting upon him: And lo a voice from heaven, saying, this is my beloved son, in whom I am well pleased.

Matthew 3:13-17

2332. Regarding the pursuit of success, you're not in competition with mankind. Rather, you're in *cooperation* with God.

For we are his workmanship, created in Christ Jesus unto good works, which God hath before ordained that we should walk in them.

Ephesians 2:10

2333. Regarding ambition, have peace in the process of pursuit.

Not that I speak in respect of want: for I have learned, in whatsoever state I am, therewith to be content. I know both how to be abased, and I know how to abound: every where and in all things I am instructed both to be full and to be hungry, both to abound and to suffer need. I can do all things through Christ, which strengtheneth me.

Philippians 4:11-13

2334. Things are not like they used to be. Times are not like they used to be. You're not like *you* used to be. As time evolves, so will you. You'll be ready for the time that is, *now*.

Thy shoes shall be iron and brass; and as thy days, so shall thy strength be.

Deuteronomy 33:25

2335. Regarding deductions, you want deductions for your taxes, but not for your *Olympics* performance in life. Jesus paid for our sins in full. However, it's our responsibility to

give our best performance daily through His grace. That's our reasonable service.

Know ye not that they, which run in a race, run all, but one receiveth the prize? So run, that ye may obtain. And every man that striveth for the mastery is temperate in all things. Now they do it to obtain a corruptible crown; but we an incorruptible. I therefore so run, not as uncertainly; so fight I, not as one that beateth the air: But I keep under my body, and bring it into subjection: lest that by any means, when I have preached to others, I myself should be a castaway.

1 Corinthians 9:24-27

2336. Regarding the time to excel and soar in life, don't run out of *airtime*. We only have a certain amount of time to shine in life. We all get a time and chance to shine. *Go for the gold!* Maximize your time to *soar!*

Whatsoever thy hand findeth to do, do it with thy might; for there is no work, nor device, nor knowledge, nor wisdom, in the grave, whither thou goest. I returned, and saw under the sun, that the race is not to the swift, nor the battle to the strong, neither yet bread to the wise, nor yet riches to men of understanding, nor yet favour to men of skill; but time and chance happeneth to them all.

Ecclesiastes 9:10-11

2337. In all labor there is profit. As we keep doing what God has put before us, He will always be pleased. We will hear him say "Well done."

I have fought a good fight, I have finished my course, I have kept the faith: henceforth there is laid up for me a crown of righteousness, which the Lord, the righteous judge, shall give me at that day: and not to me only, but unto all them also that love his appearing.

2 Timothy 4:7-8

2338. Regarding mistakes in life, if you fall, just get back up and finish your *Olympics* program. This is your lifetime opportunity. You're still a contender for the *gold medal* in life! Jesus paid it all for you. He makes you to always triumph in Him!

For a just man falleth seven times, and riseth up again: but the wicked shall fall into mischief.

Proverbs 24:16

2339. The sign of great leadership is not the maintenance of the common status quo. Rather, great leadership shows itself most apparently by the ability to create sublime productivity in the midst of chaotic uncertainty. That, my friend, has always been the source of distinction for many a great leader.

The Lord shall send the rod of thy strength out of Zion: rule thou in the midst of thine enemies.

Psalm 110:2

2340. Regarding Valentines Day, "What's good for the goose, is good for the gander". In other words, husbands love your wives, even as your own body. Happy Valentines Day!

Husbands, love your wives, even as Christ also loved the church, and gave himself for it; that he might sanctify and cleanse it with the washing of water by the word, That he might present it to himself a glorious church, not having spot, or wrinkle, or any such thing; but that it should be holy and without blemish. So ought men to love their wives as their own bodies. He that loveth his wife loveth himself. For no man ever yet hated his own flesh; but nourisheth and cherisheth it, even as the Lord the church: for we are members of his body, of his flesh, and of his bones. For this cause shall a man leave his father and mother, and shall be joined unto his wife, and they two shall be one flesh. This is a great mystery: but I speak concerning Christ and the church. Nevertheless let every one of you in particular so love his wife even as himself; and the wife see that she reverence her husband.

Ephesians 5:25-33

2341. Big fish make big waves. Sometimes when you are confident, it makes some people unsettled. They can't handle you. But, either you will be timid and not make waves, or you'll be confident and make a big difference. Big fish make big waves.

The wicked flee when no man pursueth: but the righteous are bold as a lion.

Proverbs 28:1

2342. Regarding confidence versus the opinions of people, you have to *know* that you know, that you *know*, in spite of whether people *let you know* that *they know*. Because, they *know*, and you know that they *know*, but you have to *know* that you know, in spite of whether they *let you know* that they *know*.

Do we begin again to commend ourselves? Or need we, as some others, epistles of commendation to you, or letters of commendation from you? Ye are our epistle written in our hearts, known and read of all men: forasmuch as ye are manifestly declared to be the epistle of Christ ministered by us, written not with ink, but with the spirit of the living God; not in tables of stone, but in fleshy tables of the heart.

2 Corinthians 3:1-3

2343. Excellence always rises to the top!

It pleased Darius to set over the kingdom an hundred and twenty princes, which should be over the whole kingdom; and over these three presidents; of whom Daniel was first: that the princes might give accounts unto them, and the king should have no damage. Then this Daniel was preferred above the presidents and princes, because an excellent spirit was in him; and the king thought to set him over the whole realm. Then

the presidents and princes sought to find occasion against Daniel concerning the kingdom; but they could find none occasion nor fault; forasmuch as he was faithful, neither was there any error or fault found in him.

Daniel 6:1-4

2344. Most times, the process and price of upward mobility and progress, and the people involved in that process, are not all *warm and fuzzy*. However, just like obtaining a graduate degree in university is worth it, at the end of the day, what really matters is that *piece of paper* that says, "You have successfully completed the requirements for all rights, privileges and honors pertaining to this degree."

Then came all the tribes of Israel to David unto Hebron, and spake, saying, behold, we are thy bone and thy flesh. Also in time past, when Saul was king over us, thou wast he that leddest out and broughtest in Israel: and the Lord said to thee, thou shalt feed my people Israel, and thou shalt be a captain over Israel. So all the elders of Israel came to the king to Hebron; and king David made a league with them in Hebron before the Lord: and they anointed David king over Israel. David was thirty years old when he began to reign, and he reigned forty years. In Hebron he reigned over Judah seven years and six months: and in Jerusalem he reigned thirty and three years over all Israel and Judah . . . And David went on, and grew great, and the Lord God of hosts was with him.

2 Samuel 5:1-5,10

2345. Regarding "Black History Month", for one people's history, the religious voices say "Forgive, forget, and let's move on." For another people's history, they say "Never again!" Is that not discrimination in religious expectations? We should all choose to love all people, but never forget the atrocities of history, or history may tend to try to repeat itself, unless vehemently resisted.

Open rebuke is better than secret love. Faithful are the wounds of a friend; but the kisses of an enemy are deceitful.

Proverbs 27:5-6

2346. Regarding Black History, when black citizens rise in an uproar in a city as an outcry against police brutality, murder, and racial injustices they are called "thugs" by white bigots. However, when mostly white *"fans"* tear up the city of Philadelphia after their team wins a Super Bowl, they are praised as "An enthusiastic crowd" by the news media. Is that not discrimination? The key to solving social problems is equality in evaluating the problem. Then, we can begin to see clearly how to solve them.

And why beholdest thou the mote that is in thy brother's eye, but considerest not the beam that is in thine own eye? Or how wilt thou say to thy brother, let me pull out the mote out of thine eye; and, behold, a beam is in thine own eye? Thou hypocrite, first cast out the beam out of thine own eye; and then shalt thou see clearly to cast out the mote out of thy brother's eye.

Matthew 7:3-5

2347. Some "dignified" human beings analyze, test, track, and study other human beings. We are all dignified. Yet, we all have animal-like characteristics that only the Creator has the true right to discern between or improve. The Bible is the training guide for all of God's creatures.

I said in mine heart concerning the estate of the sons of men, that God might manifest them, and that they might see that they themselves are beasts. For that which befalleth the sons of men befalleth beasts; even one thing befalleth them: as the one dieth, so dieth the other; yea, they have all one breath; so that a man hath no preeminence above a beast: for all is vanity. All go unto one place; all are of the dust, and all turn to dust again. Who knoweth the spirit of man that goeth upward, and the spirit of the beast that goeth downward to the earth? Wherefore I perceive that there is nothing better, than that a man should rejoice in his own works; for that is his portion: for who shall bring him to see what shall be after him?

Ecclesiastes 3:18-22

2348. The "Don't worry, be happy" philosophy doesn't solve any problems. Only by confronting a problem head on will you be able to eventually solve it.

Open rebuke is better than secret love. Faithful are the wounds of a friend; but the kisses of an enemy are deceitful.

Proverbs 27:5-6

2349. This is your time to rise out of the bunch, to leave the place of average, to leave the chicken coop, to soar among the clouds, and to make your mark upon history. This is your destiny as an *eagle* in life! You can do all things through Christ, which strengthens you. Rise up! It's your time to *soar*!

But they that wait upon the Lord shall renew their strength; they shall mount up with wings as eagles; they shall run, and not be weary; and they shall walk, and not faint.

Isaiah 40:31

2350. The cleanest water is obtained through distillation. God distills the greatest thoughts from the minds of a separated life. Wisdom, genius, and purity come from a sanctified life.

Through desire a man, having separated himself, seeketh and intermeddleth with all wisdom.

Proverbs 18:1

2351. Succeeding is the best thing that you can do for everyone involved in your life. Without money you are limited in the help that you can be to others.

A feast is made for laughter, and wine maketh merry: but money answereth all things.

Ecclesiastes 10:19

Distinguished Wisdom Presents . . . "Living Proverbs"–Vol.5

2352. Regarding being an employee, if you'll work like you *own* the place, act like you *own* the place, dress like you *own* the place, be early like you *own* the place, and stay late like you *own* the place, you'll eventually be *paid* like you *own* the place. You will then be qualified to own your *own* place.

And the Lord said, who then is that faithful and wise steward, whom his Lord shall make ruler over his household, to give them their portion of meat in due season? Blessed is that servant, whom his Lord when he cometh shall find so doing. Of a truth I say unto you, that he will make him ruler over all that he hath.

Luke 12:42-44

2353. Regarding the *process* of success, when you can't do everything that you want to do, do what you *can* do, and you will soon look back and see that you got a whole lot of necessary things done toward the journey.

For a dream cometh through the multitude of business; and a fool's voice is known by multitude of words.

Ecclesiastes 5:3

2354. You were born to be great, and you are. You were born to be great, and you are. You were born to be a star, and that's just what you are. You were born to be great, and you are!

Pastor Terrance Levise Turner, MBA

But ye are a chosen generation, a royal priesthood, an holy nation, a peculiar people; that ye should shew forth the praises of him who hath called you out of darkness into his marvellous light.

1 Peter 2:9

2355. Regarding change, the best time to change is *now*. Don't regret yesterday. Don't fret about what could have been, should have been, or *shouldn't* have been. Focus on today and a better tomorrow. The best time to change is now.

For he saith, I have heard thee in a time accepted, and in the day of salvation have I succoured thee: behold, now is the accepted time; behold, now is the day of salvation.

2 Corinthians 6:2

2356. *Blame*: the story of man.

And the Lord God called unto Adam, and said unto him, where art thou? And he said, I heard thy voice in the garden, and I was afraid, because I was naked; and I hid myself. And he said, who told thee that thou wast naked? Hast thou eaten of the tree, whereof I commanded thee that thou shouldest not eat? And the man said, the woman whom thou gavest to be with me, she gave me of the tree, and I did eat. And the Lord God said unto the woman, what is this that thou hast done? And the woman said, the serpent beguiled me, and I did eat. And the Lord God said unto the serpent, because thou hast done this, thou art cursed above all cattle, and above

every beast of the field; upon thy belly shalt thou go, and dust shalt thou eat all the days of thy life: and I will put enmity between thee and the woman, and between thy seed and her seed; it shall bruise thy head, and thou shalt bruise his heel. Unto the woman he said, I will greatly multiply thy sorrow and thy conception; in sorrow thou shalt bring forth children; and thy desire shall be to thy husband, and he shall rule over thee. And unto Adam he said, because thou hast hearkened unto the voice of thy wife, and hast eaten of the tree, of which I commanded thee, saying, thou shalt not eat of it: cursed is the ground for thy sake; in sorrow shalt thou eat of it all the days of thy life; thorns also and thistles shall it bring forth to thee; and thou shalt eat the herb of the field; in the sweat of thy face shalt thou eat bread, till thou return unto the ground; for out of it wast thou taken: for dust thou art, and unto dust shalt thou return. And Adam called his wife's name Eve; because she was the mother of all living. Unto Adam also and to his wife did the Lord God make coats of skins, and clothed them. And the Lord God said, behold, the man is become as one of us, to know good and evil: and now, lest he put forth his hand, and take also of the tree of life, and eat, and live for ever: therefore the Lord God sent him forth from the garden of Eden, to till the ground from whence he was taken. So he drove out the man; and he placed at the east of the Garden of Eden cherubims, and a flaming sword, which turned every way, to keep the way of the tree of life.

Genesis 3:9-24

2357. We are God's offspring. We didn't come from a *panther*, gorilla, monkey, or tadpole. We were birthed and

formed from the spirit of God. We were made to look like Him, act like Him, and reign in the earth as He reigns in the Heaven. That's liberating to know!

For in him we live, and move, and have our being; as certain also of your own poets have said, for we are also his offspring.

Acts 17:28

2358. Regarding the Olympics, at first you root for countries. Eventually, you begin to root for *excellence*. Once you become absorbed in the performance, you root for excellence. Excellence is *international*.

A gift is as a precious stone in the eyes of him that hath it: whithersoever it turneth, it prospereth.

Proverbs 17:8

2359. Regarding age, stage, and situation, don't be self-deceived concerning what's possible. Neither, be convinced of what's impossible.

Whatsoever thy hand findeth to do, do it with thy might; for there is no work, nor device, nor knowledge, nor wisdom, in the grave, whither thou goest. I returned, and saw under the sun, that the race is not to the swift, nor the battle to the strong, neither yet bread to the wise, nor yet riches to men of understanding, nor yet favour to men of skill; but time and chance happeneth to them all.

Ecclesiastes 9:10-11

2360. The style of a victor is *"sweat-less success."*

But none of these things move me, neither count I my life dear unto myself, so that I might finish my course with joy, and the ministry, which I have received of the Lord Jesus, to testify the gospel of the grace of God.

Acts 20:24

2361. Concerning a harvest, it's work to prep the ground. It's work to plant the ground. It's work to tend the field. It's work to get in the harvest. Then, it's work to maintain the harvest. It's *work! Work! Work! Work! Work*! And it's worth it!

He that tilleth his land shall be satisfied with bread: but he that followeth vain persons is void of understanding.

Proverbs 12:11

2362. Regarding sales and marketing, if you don't sow, you will never *know*. The only way to know is to *sow*. You will *reap* what you *sow*.

There is that scattereth, and yet increaseth; and there is that withholdeth more than is meet, but it tendeth to poverty. The liberal soul shall be made fat: and he that watereth shall be watered also himself.

Proverbs 11:24-25

Pastor Terrance Levise Turner, MBA

2363. Love your neighbor as you love yourself, but be sure to *love yourself*.

He that getteth wisdom loveth his own soul: he that keepeth understanding shall find good.

Proverbs 19:8

2364. Whatever you're facing today, take time to encourage yourself in the Lord by rejoicing in thanksgiving *everyday*!

Rejoice in the Lord always: and again I say, rejoice. Let your moderation be known unto all men. The Lord is at hand. Be careful for nothing; but in every thing by prayer and supplication with thanksgiving let your requests be made known unto God. And the peace of God, which passeth all understanding, shall keep your hearts and minds through Christ Jesus. Finally, brethren, whatsoever things are true, whatsoever things are honest, whatsoever things are just, whatsoever things are pure, whatsoever things are lovely, whatsoever things are of good report; if there be any virtue, and if there be any praise, think on these things. Those things, which ye have both learned, and received, and heard, and seen in me, do: and the God of peace shall be with you.

Philippians 4:4-9

2365. Give thanks. It feels better.

Trust in the Lord, and do good; so shalt thou dwell in the land, and verily thou shalt be fed. Delight thyself also in the Lord:

and he shall give thee the desires of thine heart. Commit thy way unto the Lord; trust also in him; and he shall bring it to pass. And he shall bring forth thy righteousness as the light, and thy judgment as the noonday.

Psalm 37:3-6

2366. Concerning challenges, you have to learn to "make a *mole-hill* out of a mountain." You have to change your vision of the problem, and you will bring it down to size. You can do all things through Christ, which strengthens you. If you change your perspective of the challenge, you can conquer it.

And David left his carriage in the hand of the keeper of the carriage, and ran into the army, and came and saluted his brethren. And as he talked with them, behold, there came up the champion, the Philistine of Gath, Goliath by name, out of the armies of the Philistines, and spake according to the same words: and David heard them. And all the men of Israel, when they saw the man, fled from him, and were sore afraid. And the men of Israel said, have ye seen this man that is come up? Surely to defy Israel is he come up: and it shall be, that the man who killeth him, the king will enrich him with great riches, and will give him his daughter, and make his father's house free in Israel. And David spake to the men that stood by him, saying, what shall be done to the man that killeth this Philistine, and taketh away the reproach from Israel? For who is this uncircumcised Philistine, that he should defy the armies of the living God? And the people answered him after this manner, saying, so shall it be done to the man that killeth him. And Eliab his eldest brother heard when he spake unto

the men; and Eliab's anger was kindled against David, and he said, why camest thou down hither? And with whom hast thou left those few sheep in the wilderness? I know thy pride, and the naughtiness of thine heart; for thou art come down that thou mightest see the battle. And David said, what have I now done? Is there not a cause? And he turned from him toward another, and spake after the same manner: and the people answered him again after the former manner. And when the words were heard which David spake, they rehearsed them before Saul: and he sent for him. And David said to Saul, let no man's heart fail because of him; thy servant will go and fight with this Philistine.

1 Samuel 17:22-32

2367. You are an optimum, excellent, superior, outstanding, godly, exceptional person. You fulfill God's highest ideals. You're pleasing to God. He loves you very much. He wishes above all things that you prosper, and be in good health, even as your soul prospers. And He desires for you to have a long, exceptional, and fulfilling life. You are blessed.

I will praise thee; for I am fearfully and wonderfully made: marvellous are thy works; and that my soul knoweth right well.

Psalm 139:14

2368. Here's a key to ongoing success: Make a list. Work your list. Repeat.

And the Lord answered me, and said, write the vision, and make it plain upon tables, That he may run that readeth it. For the vision is yet for an appointed time, but at the end it shall speak, and not lie: though it tarry, wait for it; because it will surely come, it will not tarry. Behold, his soul, which is lifted up, is not upright in him: but the just shall live by his faith.

Habakkuk 2:2-4

2369. If you want to be successful and stay encouraged, then, you must develop a highly refined, selective filter. You must learn how to filter out the negative comments and experiences, while snagging, clinging to, and treasuring the positive and affirming.

And David left his carriage in the hand of the keeper of the carriage, and ran into the army, and came and saluted his brethren. And as he talked with them, behold, there came up the champion, the Philistine of Gath, Goliath by name, out of the armies of the Philistines, and spake according to the same words: and David heard them. And all the men of Israel, when they saw the man, fled from him, and were sore afraid. And the men of Israel said, have ye seen this man that is come up? Surely to defy Israel is he come up: and it shall be, that the man who killeth him, the king will enrich him with great riches, and will give him his daughter, and make his father's house free in Israel. And David spake to the men that stood by him, saying, what shall be done to the man that killeth this Philistine, and taketh away the reproach from Israel? For who is this uncircumcised Philistine, that he should defy the armies of the living God? And the people answered him after

this manner, saying, so shall it be done to the man that killeth him. And Eliab his eldest brother heard when he spake unto the men; and Eliab's anger was kindled against David, and he said, why camest thou down hither? And with whom hast thou left those few sheep in the wilderness? I know thy pride, and the naughtiness of thine heart; for thou art come down that thou mightest see the battle. And David said, what have I now done? Is there not a cause? And he turned from him toward another, and spake after the same manner: and the people answered him again after the former manner. And when the words were heard which David spake, they rehearsed them before Saul: and he sent for him. And David said to Saul, let no man's heart fail because of him; thy servant will go and fight with this Philistine.

> 1 Samuel 17:22-32

2370. The Bible is a message of renewal. God has used various carriers and preservers of His knowledge in order to renew our relationship with Him. God loves all people. He loved us all from the beginning. His love for us existed far before the *love-letter* of the Bible was transcribed to us by those who experienced His love. You are God's son or daughter. You are God's offspring. He so loves *you* today!

Knowing this first, that no prophecy of the scripture is of any private interpretation. For the prophecy came not in old time by the will of man: but holy men of God spake as they were moved by the Holy Ghost.

> 2 Peter 1:20-21

2371. Thank God for the life and ministry of Dr. Billy Graham and other faithful ministers of the Gospel of the Lord Jesus Christ. He helped to empty out Hell, and to instead, populate Heaven during his lifetime. He served his generation, and generations to come. Every soul saved through his ministry has the potential of saving other souls, and multiplying into eternity, all to the glory of God.

I have fought a good fight, I have finished my course, I have kept the faith: henceforth there is laid up for me a crown of righteousness, which the Lord, the righteous judge, shall give me at that day: and not to me only, but unto all them also that love his appearing.

2 Timothy 4:7-8

2372. It's ok to have questions about your faith. An *unquestioned* faith is an unexamined faith. Faith is purest and most sincere in the absence of certain obvious evidences. If you can continue to passionately pursue your faith, and sacrifice and represent your Lord in the midst of uncertainty, you will receive the greater reward.

Now faith is the substance of things hoped for, the evidence of things not seen. For by it the elders obtained a good report. But without faith it is impossible to please him: for he that cometh to God must believe that he is, and that he is a rewarder of them that diligently seek him.

Hebrews 11:1-2,6

2373. When your faith is shaken, and when you have questions about the certainties of life, then, go back to the Bible. Read several chapters the Bible daily. God's Word will build up your faith in the certainties of life. God's Word is truth.

So then faith cometh by hearing, and hearing by the word of God.

Romans 10:17

2374. God is God. God never changes. God's laws never change. Therefore, we should learn to live by His laws, and work His laws to our favor. If we do, we will have unstinting success. God's laws never change. God never changes. He's faithful to His laws. His laws are for our good. *Always.*

God is not a man, that he should lie; neither the son of man, that he should repent: hath he said, and shall he not do it? Or hath he spoken, and shall he not make it good? Behold, I have received commandment to bless: and he hath blessed; and I cannot reverse it.

Numbers 23:19-20

2375. Regarding how to worry less, you should always assume the best, until proven otherwise. You will save yourself a lot of worry-time.

Rejoice in the Lord alway: and again I say, rejoice. Let your moderation be known unto all men. The Lord is at hand. Be

careful for nothing; but in every thing by prayer and supplication with thanksgiving let your requests be made known unto God. And the peace of God, which passeth all understanding, shall keep your hearts and minds through Christ Jesus. Finally, brethren, whatsoever things are true, whatsoever things are honest, whatsoever things are just, whatsoever things are pure, whatsoever things are lovely, whatsoever things are of good report; if there be any virtue, and if there be any praise, think on these things. Those things, which ye have both learned, and received, and heard, and seen in me, do: and the God of peace shall be with you.

Philippians 4:4-9

2376. Don't worry. His eye is on the sparrow, and He certainly watches over you.

Are not two sparrows sold for a farthing? And one of them shall not fall on the ground without your father. But the very hairs of your head are all numbered. Fear ye not therefore, ye are of more value than many sparrows.

Matthew 10:29-31

2377. "Dear Heavenly Father, me and my family are an one of a kind opportunity for You to fulfill Your covenant promises in the earth. We are a prime opportunity for You to have a good name in the earth. We have obeyed Your Word. We have believed in Your Son, Jesus Christ. We have supported your kingdom through giving tithes and offerings. Now, I pray, that your kingdom come. Your will be done, in

Earth, as it is in Heaven. Bless us indeed, according to your promises. Make our name great in the earth. Bless those who bless us, and make us a blessing in the earth. I pray this, in Jesus name, amen."

Now the Lord had said unto Abram, get thee out of thy country, and from thy kindred, and from thy father's house, unto a land that I will shew thee: and I will make of thee a great nation, and I will bless thee, and make thy name great; and thou shalt be a blessing: and I will bless them that bless thee, and curse him that curseth thee: and in thee shall all families of the earth be blessed.

Genesis 12:1-3

2378. Study and practice will equal better performance.

And that ye study to be quiet, and to do your own business, and to work with your own hands, as we commanded you; that ye may walk honestly toward them that are without, and that ye may have lack of nothing.

1 Thessalonians 4:11-12

2379. Regarding relationships, some things you choose to do for peace sake. Some things you refuse to do for principle sake.

If it be possible, as much as lieth in you, live peaceably with all men.

Romans 12:18

2380. Keep doing great things, and congratulate yourself along the way.

The desire accomplished is sweet to the soul ...

Proverbs 13:19a

2381. Regular study, plus, regular practice, will equal extraordinary performance.

If the iron be blunt, and he do not whet the edge, then must he put to more strength: but wisdom is profitable to direct.

Ecclesiastes 10:10

2382. Focus and concentration is the price of success. It's required.

Seest thou a man diligent in his business? He shall stand before kings; he shall not stand before mean men.

Proverbs 22:29

2383. Prayer relieves your silent concerns.

Rejoice in the Lord alway: and again I say, rejoice. Let your moderation be known unto all men. The Lord is at hand. Be careful for nothing; but in every thing by prayer and supplication with thanksgiving let your requests be made known unto God. And the peace of God, which passeth all understanding, shall keep your hearts and minds through Christ Jesus. Finally, brethren, whatsoever things are true,

whatsoever things are honest, whatsoever things are just, whatsoever things are pure, whatsoever things are lovely, whatsoever things are of good report; if there be any virtue, and if there be any praise, think on these things. Those things, which ye have both learned, and received, and heard, and seen in me, do: and the God of peace shall be with you.

Philippians 4:4-9

2384. Life is often so busy on a regular basis, that when life slows you down, it seems like you should be doing something else. However, you are actually doing what you really need to be doing. *Rest* is an accomplishment too!

And he said unto them, come ye yourselves apart into a desert place, and rest a while: for there were many coming and going, and they had no leisure so much as to eat.

Mark 6:31

2385. In life, you have to try to play the best hand that you have been given. However, at the end of the day, life will have the *final draw*.

The lot is cast into the lap; but the whole disposing thereof is of the Lord.

Proverbs 16:33

2386. A regular prayer-life is just like exercising. If you just let it go, and stop praying, then, your life will begin to sag and

get out of shape, and eventually fall apart. However, through a regular prayer-life, you can keep your life fit, and looking like a champion!

And he spake a parable unto them *to this end*, that men ought always to pray, and not to faint.

> Luke 18:1

2387. Success is obtained through aspirations, inspiration, inclinations, education, preparation, and dedication.

For a dream cometh through the multitude of business; and a fool's voice is known by multitude of words.

> Ecclesiastes 5:3

2388. Don't just take what's forecasted in your life. Rather, pray. Things will happen whether or whether not you pray. Prayer will determine whether or whether not certain things happen. Your prayers will determine what happens, regardless of the forecast or whether.

Confess your faults one to another, and pray one for another, that ye may be healed. The effectual fervent prayer of a righteous man availeth much. Elias was a man subject to like passions as we are, and he prayed earnestly that it might not rain: and it rained not on the earth by the space of three years and six months. And he prayed again, and the heaven gave rain, and the earth brought forth her fruit.

> James 5:16-18

2389. Even if you are a lion, don't wrestle alligators in the *swamp*. Wait until you get them on land. Take time to do a S.W.O.T analysis of your situation. Recognize your strengths, weaknesses, opportunities, and threats. Determine how you can maximize your advantages. Then, choose your battles.

Or what king, going to make war against another king, sitteth not down first, and consulteth whether he be able with ten thousand to meet him that cometh against him with twenty thousand? Or else, while the other is yet a great way off, he sendeth an ambassage, and desireth conditions of peace. So likewise, whosoever he be of you that forsaketh not all that he hath, he cannot be my disciple.

Luke 14:31-33

2390. No matter who you are, no matter how rich or poor, no matter how healthy or not, success or failure, riches or poverty, health or sickness, life or death, are only separated by a tenuous thread called *chance* and the unbreakable, always available bond of life called God's mercy. But, be encouraged, because whosoever calls upon the name of the Lord shall be saved.

Whatsoever thy hand findeth to do, do it with thy might; for there is no work, nor device, nor knowledge, nor wisdom, in the grave, whither thou goest. I returned, and saw under the sun, that the race is not to the swift, nor the battle to the strong, neither yet bread to the wise, nor yet riches to men of understanding, nor yet favour to men of skill; but time and chance happeneth to them all.

Ecclesiastes 9:10-11

2391. A complaining wife reminds a husband of all of his potential to do better. However, a *nagging* wife negates that potential. Results are determined by how requests are presented.

As an earring of gold, and an ornament of fine gold, so is a wise reprover upon an obedient ear.

Proverbs 25:12

2392. You are the architect of your own future, and God has given you the power to prosper! An architect is a person whose profession is to design plans for buildings, bridges, etc., and to generally administer the construction of those projects. They are the planner, builder, and creator. You are responsible for planning your future success. You can attain your plans through God's grace, strength, and guidance.

A man's heart deviseth his way: but the Lord directeth his steps.

Proverbs 16:9

2393. If you continue to learn usable knowledge, and continue to practice what you've learned, you will become like a mother who is pregnant with a full-term baby. You won't be able to keep the success that has been formed inside of you from making its *grand exit* to the outside world. You will have to give birth to the success that you have *become*!

Cast thy bread upon the waters: for thou shalt find it after many days. Give a portion to seven, and also to eight; for thou knowest not what evil shall be upon the earth. If the clouds be full of rain, they empty themselves upon the earth: and if the tree fall toward the south, or toward the north, in the place where the tree falleth, there it shall be. He that observeth the wind shall not sow; and he that regardeth the clouds shall not reap. As thou knowest not what is the way of the spirit, nor how the bones do grow in the womb of her that is with child: even so thou knowest not the works of God who maketh all. In the morning sow thy seed, and in the evening withhold not thine hand: for thou knowest not whether shall prosper, either this or that, or whether they both shall be alike good.

Ecclesiastes 11:1-6

2394. Don't worry about what didn't get done. Don't worry about the battle that wasn't won. Don't worry about tasks of yesterday. Just start again today, and do it the right way.

So teach us to number our days, that we may apply our hearts unto wisdom.

Psalm 90:12

2395. The salve of love helps to heal the soul. It makes you feel better. It makes you feel whole. Thank God for marriage. Thank God for devotion. It's like a medicine of miracle. It's God's relationship potion. From the holy mix of two comes a better you. Holy matrimony between a man and woman

creates a miracle that's truly uncommon. God bless the two that said, "I do."

And he answered and said unto them, have ye not read, that he which made them at the beginning made them male and female, and said, for this cause shall a man leave father and mother, and shall cleave to his wife: and they twain shall be one flesh? Wherefore they are no more twain, but one flesh. What therefore God hath joined together, let not man put asunder.

Matthew 19:4-6

2396. If your boss or customers are saying you're doing a good job, then, you can take that to the bank. If others, who are not paying you, have words of criticism, then, you can take that to the *trash*. Only focus on the words of paying customers, or the one's who hired you.

He that is despised, and hath a servant, is better than he that honoureth himself, and lacketh bread.

Proverbs 12:9

2397. You are a unique expression of God in the earth. You are God's direct offspring. You have a unique personality that pleases God. He is fascinated with watching Himself uniquely expressed through you. You are very special. You are fearfully and wonderfully made! Always love and appreciate yourself as God's special handiwork.

And God said, let us make man in our image, after our likeness: and let them have dominion over the fish of the sea, and over the fowl of the air, and over the cattle, and over all the earth, and over every creeping thing that creepeth upon the earth. So God created man in his own image, in the image of God created he him; male and female created he them. And God blessed them, and God said unto them, be fruitful, and multiply, and replenish the earth, and subdue it: and have dominion over the fish of the sea, and over the fowl of the air, and over every living thing that moveth upon the earth.

Genesis 1:26-28

2398. Religion and other nefarious agendas discount you in order to control and subdue you. However, the true wisdom of God always builds you up. Always discern the difference.

Who also hath made us able ministers of the new testament; not of the letter, but of the spirit: for the letter killeth, but the spirit giveth life.

2 Corinthians 3:6

2399. Rejoice in the Lord always, and again I say, rejoice! Rejoice and sing by choice. No matter what the *weather* in life may be. You will feel better. Day or night you'll see the light!

Rejoice in the Lord alway: and again I say, rejoice.

Philippians 4:4

2400. Regarding relationships, you don't always have to burn bridges. However, it's sometimes necessary to cross an *alternate bridge* to get to where you need to be. New bridges are often necessary to get to the new places God has for you in life. Excepting the more serious covenant of marriage, if you're not completely satisfied with a situation, and you have previously appealed the other party to remedy your concerns, then, you owe it to yourself to explore other options.

So he departed thence, and found Elisha the son of Shaphat, who was plowing with twelve yoke of oxen before him, and he with the twelfth: and Elijah passed by him, and cast his mantle upon him. And he left the oxen, and ran after Elijah, and said, let me, I pray thee, kiss my father and my mother, and then I will follow thee. And he said unto him, go back again: for what have I done to thee? And he returned back from him, and took a yoke of oxen, and slew them, and boiled their flesh with the instruments of the oxen, and gave unto the people, and they did eat. Then he arose, and went after Elijah, and ministered unto him.

1 Kings 19:19-21

2401. When faced with unfair behavior from others, then, do not fret. God is a righteous and all-seeing judge. He will reward every person according to his or her works. He will defend you. God is our refuge and strength. He is a very present help in trouble.

Truly my soul waiteth upon God: from him cometh my salvation. He only is my rock and my salvation; he is my

defence; I shall not be greatly moved. How long will ye imagine mischief against a man? Ye shall be slain all of you: as a bowing wall shall ye be, and as a tottering fence. They only consult to cast him down from his excellency: they delight in lies: they bless with their mouth, but they curse inwardly. Selah. My soul, wait thou only upon God; for my expectation is from him. He only is my rock and my salvation: he is my defence; I shall not be moved. In God is my salvation and my glory: the rock of my strength, and my refuge, is in God. Trust in him at all times; ye people, pour out your heart before him: God is a refuge for us. Selah. Surely men of low degree are vanity, and men of high degree are a lie: to be laid in the balance, they are altogether lighter than vanity. Trust not in oppression, and become not vain in robbery: if riches increase, set not your heart upon them. God hath spoken once; twice have I heard this; that power belongeth unto God. Also unto thee, O Lord, belongeth mercy: for thou renderest to every man according to his work.

Psalm 62

2402. True humility need not boast *nor bow*. Humility is simply reality. You know who you are, and you know who others are. Thus, you just be yourself.

I have said, ye are gods; and all of you are children of the Most High.

Psalm 82:6

2403. Uncommon ideas come at common times. However, only the uncommon have the uncommon sense to recognize them for the uncommon value they potentially contain. Moreover, uncommon, is the person who has the uncommon tenacity to *mine* the treasure until the full value is extracted. Here's the lesson: Don't let your treasure go undiscovered, unrecognized, and unrealized.

The slothful man roasteth not that which he took in hunting: but the substance of a diligent man is precious.

Proverbs 12:27

2404. Regarding your problems, you have to know that God is greater. He has to be, because He is the Creator. Before the problem existed, He has the solution. Therefore, the argument is not can He, but *will* He? The argument only remains if you are unaware or unsure of His love. So, let's settle the argument: God knows, God can, and God will, because God is the Creator. God is greater. God is love. And most importantly, God loves you! It's settled. Amen.

Hast thou not known? Hast thou not heard, that the everlasting God, the Lord, the creator of the ends of the earth, fainteth not, neither is weary? There is no searching of his understanding. He giveth power to the faint; and to them that have no might he increaseth strength. Even the youths shall faint and be weary, and the young men shall utterly fall: but they that wait upon the Lord shall renew their strength; they shall mount up with wings as eagles; they shall run, and not be weary; and they shall walk, and not faint.

Isaiah 40:28-31

2405. Take care of the problems. Go ahead and solve them. Do what you need to, because our God is with you.

God is our refuge and strength, a very present help in trouble.

Psalm 46:1

2406. Regarding impending trouble, go ahead and repair the roof while it's still *partly cloudy*!

A prudent man foreseeth the evil, and hideth himself; but the simple pass on, and are punished.

Proverbs 27:12

2407. In regard to the *"good fight of faith"*, the Word always works. Prayer always works. Worship always works. Confession always works. It will help you walk through the seasons of your life. You can fight the good fight of faith through the season. However, your faith will not change the season. Your faith will help you make it through the season. Yet, if it's the dead of Winter, then, your faith won't change the season to Spring. The seasons change on their own. However, the *good fight of faith* helps you to maintain your faith and joy no matter what the season is.

To every thing there is a season, and a time to every purpose under the heaven:

A time to be born, and a time to die;

A time to plant, and a time to pluck up that, which is planted;

A time to kill, and a time to heal;

A time to break down, and a time to build up;

A time to weep, and a time to laugh;

A time to mourn, and a time to dance;

A time to cast away stones,

And a time to gather stones together;

A time to embrace, and a time to refrain from embracing;

A time to get, and a time to lose;

A time to keep, and a time to cast away;

A time to rend, and a time to sew;

A time to keep silence, and a time to speak;

A time to love, and a time to hate;

A time of war, and a time of peace.

Ecclesiastes 3:1-8

2408. If you want favor, then, do those things that please the Lord. If you want *more* favor, then, do *more* things that please the Lord.

He that diligently seeketh good procureth favour: but he that seeketh mischief, it shall come unto him.

Proverbs 11:27

2409. Regarding marketing, the best customers to have are the one's that *buy*.

These were more noble than those in Thessalonica, in that they received the word with all readiness of mind, and searched the scriptures daily, whether those things were so. Therefore many of them believed; also of honourable women, which were Greeks, and of men, not a few.

Acts 17:11-12

2410. Diligence doesn't discriminate. Through *better service* is "*How The West Was Won?*"

The hand of the diligent shall bear rule: but the slothful shall be under tribute.

Proverbs 12:24

2411. Turn your complaints into prayers. Direct them to the One that can solve them.

Rejoice in the Lord alway: and again I say, rejoice. Let your moderation be known unto all men. The Lord is at hand. Be careful for nothing; but in every thing by prayer and supplication with thanksgiving let your requests be made known unto God. And the peace of God, which passeth all understanding, shall keep your hearts and minds through Christ Jesus. Finally, brethren, whatsoever things are true, whatsoever things are honest, whatsoever things are just, whatsoever things are pure, whatsoever things are lovely, whatsoever things are of good report; if there be any virtue, and if there be any praise, think on these things. Those things, which ye have both learned, and received, and heard, and seen in me, do: and the God of peace shall be with you.

Philippians 4:4-9

2412. Regarding your legacy, see your life as *perpetual*. You're living now to help someone else live better later. You're learning now to help someone else know better later.

Only take heed to thyself, and keep thy soul diligently, lest thou forget the things, which thine eyes have seen, and lest they depart from thy heart all the days of thy life: but teach them thy sons, and thy sons' sons.

Deuteronomy 4:9

2413. Peace is very important. It's tangible. However, you often don't notice it until you lose it.

Pastor Terrance Levise Turner, MBA

And into whatsoever city or town ye shall enter, enquire who in it is worthy; and there abide till ye go thence. And when ye come into an house, salute it. And if the house be worthy, let your peace come upon it: but if it be not worthy, let your peace return to you. And whosoever shall not receive you, nor hear your words, when ye depart out of that house or city, shake off the dust of your feet.

Matthew 10:11-14

2414. Don't worry! God has already blessed you, and there's nothing the devil can do about it! God has surrounded you with protection, blessing, and favor. He is protecting your family, prospering your job or business, and everything you have on every side. And you are increasing in wealth and wisdom! In Jesus name, amen!

Hast not thou made an hedge about him, and about his house, and about all that he hath on every side? Thou hast blessed the work of his hands, and his substance is increased in the land.

Job 1:10

2415. In every person's life, there is a season where you do what you *have* to do for a living. The goal is to get to the season where you can do what you *want* to do for a living.

And whatsoever ye do, do it heartily, as to the Lord, and not unto men; knowing that of the Lord ye shall receive the reward of the inheritance: for ye serve the Lord Christ.

Colossians 3:23-24

2416. It's *not* crowded at the top, because *few* people do what's necessary to get to the top.

Because strait is the gate, and narrow is the way, which leadeth unto life, and few there be that find it.

Matthew 7:14

2417. No matter how dark it becomes in the world, the darkness can never extinguish the Light. Light always vanquishes darkness. Don't pray for an escape out of the darkness of the world. Rather, shine *brighter*! You are the *light* of the world!

Ye are the salt of the earth: but if the salt have lost his savour, wherewith shall it be salted? It is thenceforth good for nothing, but to be cast out, and to be trodden under foot of men. Ye are the light of the world. A city that is set on an hill cannot be hid. Neither do men light a candle, and put it under a bushel, but on a candlestick; and it giveth light unto all that are in the house. Let your light so shine before men, that they may see your good works, and glorify your father, which is in heaven.

Matthew 5:13-16

2418. If you can stand the risk of being embarrassed and misunderstood, then, you can possibly become great.

Pastor Terrance Levise Turner, MBA

And he went out from thence, and came into his own country; and his disciples follow him. And when the sabbath day was come, he began to teach in the synagogue: and many hearing him were astonished, saying, from whence hath this man these things? And what wisdom is this, which is given unto him, that even such mighty works are wrought by his hands? Is not this the carpenter, the son of Mary, the brother of James, and Joses, and of Juda, and Simon? And are not his sisters here with us? And they were offended at him. But Jesus, said unto them, A prophet is not without honour, but in his own country, and among his own kin, and in his own house. And he could there do no mighty work, save that he laid his hands upon a few sick folk, and healed them. And he marvelled because of their unbelief. And he went round about the villages, teaching.

Mark 6:1-6

2419. Regarding righteousness, you have the power to change your circumstances. Don't let your circumstances change you. Shape your environment. Don't let your environment shape you.

I beseech you therefore, brethren, by the mercies of God, that ye present your bodies a living sacrifice, holy, acceptable unto God, which is your reasonable service. And be not conformed to this world: but be ye transformed by the renewing of your mind, that ye may prove what is that good, and acceptable, and perfect, will of God.

Romans 12:1-2

2420. Patience has always won the battle.

He that is slow to anger is better than the mighty; and he that ruleth his spirit than he that taketh a city.

Proverbs 16:32

2421. Regarding taking advice from friends, only take counsel from those who are in the "know" and/or who are in the "*dough!*"

Buy the truth, and sell it not; also wisdom, and instruction, and understanding.

Proverbs 23:23

2422. The cure for poverty is knowledge and correction.

The ransom of a man's life are his riches: but the poor heareth not rebuke.

Proverbs 13:8

2423. Entertainment has a limited time before its value decreases. Truth has timeless value.

There are many devices in a man's heart; nevertheless the counsel of the Lord, that shall stand.

Proverbs 19:21

2424. The only direction for your life now is *up*! You have gone through too many changes, processes, and transitions to ever go back down to a lower state. An oak tree could never be forced back inside of the shell of an acorn!

As thou knowest not what is the way of the spirit, nor how the bones do grow in the womb of her that is with child: even so thou knowest not the works of God who maketh all. In the morning sow thy seed, and in the evening withhold not thine hand: for thou knowest not whether shall prosper, either this or that, or whether they both shall be alike good.

Ecclesiastes 11:5-6

2425. History always eventually reveals its secrets. Whether, in life, at the grave, or through archeological finds, history always eventually reveals its secrets. So, you always want to let your actions line up on the favorable side of history. Choose love. Choose justice. Choose truth.

I call heaven and earth to record this day against you, that I have set before you life and death, blessing and cursing: therefore choose life, that both thou and thy seed may live.

Deuteronomy 30:19

2426. Regarding your reward for using your gifts to bless others, a water hose in use can't help but to get wet.

There is that scattereth, and yet increaseth; and there is that withholdeth more than is meet, but it tendeth to poverty. The

liberal soul shall be made fat: and he that watereth shall be watered also himself.

Proverbs 11:24-25

2427. As you go forth into your *work-along-day*, be sure to have taken time to sharpen your *axe*! Sharpen your *mind*. Meditate God's Word, pray, and worship. It will make your daily work-life so much smoother and more effective.

If the iron be blunt, and he do not whet the edge, then must he put to more strength: but wisdom is profitable to direct.

Ecclesiastes 10:10

2428. After you've done your part to run your part of the world, leave the rest in God's hands.

The heaven, even the heavens, are the Lord's: but the earth hath he given to the children of men.

Psalm 115:16

2429. Do it *now*! Because "One day I'm gonna. . ." will soon be a "*goner!*"

Whatsoever thy hand findeth to do, do it with thy might; for there is no work, nor device, nor knowledge, nor wisdom, in the grave, whither thou goest. I returned, and saw under the sun, that the race is not to the swift, nor the battle to the strong, neither yet bread to the wise, nor yet riches to men of understanding, nor yet favour to men of skill; but time and

chance happeneth to them all. For man also knoweth not his time: as the fishes that are taken in an evil net, and as the birds that are caught in the snare; so are the sons of men snared in an evil time, when it falleth suddenly upon them. This wisdom have I seen also under the sun, and it seemed great unto me.

Ecclesiastes 9:10-13

2430. The appeal of some popular preaching is a combination of inspired experience and carnal charisma. They inspire the inexperienced and cater to the carnal listener's feelings.

The simple believeth every word: but the prudent man looketh well to his going.

Proverbs 14:15

2431. In today's reality television society, *raggedy* may be acceptable. However, excellence is always preferred.

Then this Daniel was preferred above the presidents and princes, because an excellent spirit was in him; and the king thought to set him over the whole realm.

Daniel 6:3

2432. When people who don't usually contact you suddenly contact you for no particular reason, then, you can be sure that there is usually a very specific reason, even if the reason is not initially spoken.

The simple believeth every word: but the prudent man looketh well to his going.

Proverbs 14:15

2433. A Christian should be a book that people can *"judge by its cover."* If people can't tell what you're about by an obvious glance or interaction, they possibly won't believe the "Author and Finisher" of your faith long enough to spend time experiencing the whole book! Be a living story others can believe in. Be an example!

Do we begin again to commend ourselves? Or need we, as some others, epistles of commendation to you, or letters of commendation from you? Ye are our epistle written in our hearts, known and read of all men: forasmuch as ye are manifestly declared to be the epistle of Christ ministered by us, written not with ink, but with the spirit of the living God; not in tables of stone, but in fleshy tables of the heart.

2 Corinthians 3:1-3

2434. Take the rough edges of your natural gifts, talents, and advantages, and begin to chip away your doubts and fears through applying your faith to overcome the hard places of life, thus, sharpening what you've got left to work with. Then, launch those skills like an arrow toward the target of a fervently focused desired outcome, and you will surely hit the bull's-eye of a successful future! You can do it. You have time, if you focus *now*!

Pastor Terrance Levise Turner, MBA

If the iron be blunt, and he do not whet the edge, then must he put to more strength: but wisdom is profitable to direct.

Ecclesiastes 10:10

2435. Business leadership and dominance has more to do with strategy and timing, rather than, *sheer hustle*. The right strategy and the right timing can advantage you to bring your opponent to its knees with the minimal amount of wasted force or resources, just like an expert martial artist who knows when, where, how, and what to exert pressure upon to master his or her opponent. Success in business and life takes strategy and skill.

Wisdom is good with an inheritance: and by it there is profit to them that see the sun. For wisdom is a defence, and money is a defence: but the excellency of knowledge is, that wisdom giveth life to them that have it.

Ecclesiastes 7:11-12

2436. Parents, teachers, and students be aware of the student that is now called "Class clown", because he or she now have the perfect ingredients for the making of a highly paid actor, comedian, or movie star. Be aware of how you handle the student that you now call "Nerd', because he or she currently have the ingredients to one day be on the *Forbes Top 100 Billionaires List*. Be aware that all finished *masterpieces* started as ingredients. What determines the outcome is the level of discernment of the teachers and the degree of skillful mastery in the preparation of the pupil.

And Moses was learned in all the wisdom of the Egyptians, and was mighty in words and in deeds. And when he was full forty years old, it came into his heart to visit his brethren the children of Israel. And seeing one of them suffer wrong, he defended him, and avenged him that was oppressed, and smote the Egyptian: for he supposed his brethren would have understood how that God by his hand would deliver them: but they understood not. And the next day he shewed himself unto them as they strove, and would have set them at one again, saying, sirs, ye are brethren; why do ye wrong one to another? But he that did his neighbour wrong thrust him away, saying, who made thee a ruler and a judge over us? Wilt thou kill me, as thou diddest the Egyptian yesterday? Then fled Moses at this saying, and was a stranger in the land of Madian, where he begat two sons. And when forty years were expired, there appeared to him in the wilderness of mount Sina an angel of the Lord in a flame of fire in a bush. When Moses saw it, he wondered at the sight: and as he drew near to behold it, the voice of the Lord came unto him, saying, I am the God of thy fathers, the God of Abraham, and the God of Isaac, and the God of Jacob. Then Moses trembled, and durst not behold. Then said the Lord to him, put off thy shoes from thy feet: for the place where thou standest is holy ground. I have seen, I have seen the affliction of my people, which is in Egypt, and I have heard their groaning, and am come down to deliver them. And now come, I will send thee into Egypt. This Moses whom they refused, saying, who made thee a ruler and a judge? The same did God send to be a ruler and a deliverer by the hand of the angel, which appeared to him in the bush.

Acts 7:22-35

2437. Keep on worshipping God. Create your own environment, atmosphere, and *force field*. No one can interfere with a worshipping heart.

For thus saith the high and lofty one that inhabiteth eternity, whose name is holy; I dwell in the high and holy place, with him also that is of a contrite and humble spirit, to revive the spirit of the humble, and to revive the heart of the contrite ones.

Isaiah 57:15

2438. Encouragement is oxygen to the soul. In this world, there is so much that is trying to take your breath away! Therefore, it's good to continually revive yourself with words, music, and laughter for encouragement.

Let the word of Christ dwell in you richly in all wisdom; teaching and admonishing one another in psalms and hymns and spiritual songs, singing with grace in your hearts to the Lord.

Colossians 3:16

2439. "It ain't as bad as you think. It will look better in the morning."

General Colin Powell
(Rule # 1 of his "Thirteen Rules" from the book It Worked For Me)

For his anger endureth but a moment; in his favour is life: weeping may endure for a night, but joy cometh in the morning.

Psalm 30:5

2440. If it sounds good, but looks bad, always listen to your eyes.

The simple believeth every word: but the prudent man looketh well to his going.

Proverbs 14:15

2441. The person who has control of his or her own spirit has control of the situation.

In your patience possess ye your souls.

Luke 21:19

2442. Marriage should be a personal mutual admiration society between a husband and wife.

Tell me, O thou whom my soul loveth, where thou feedest, where thou makest thy flock to rest at noon: for why should I be as one that turneth aside by the flocks of thy companions? If thou know not, O thou fairest among women, go thy way forth by the footsteps of the flock, and feed thy kids beside the shepherds' tents. I have compared thee, O my love, to a company of horses in Pharaoh's chariots. Thy cheeks are comely with rows of jewels, thy neck with chains of gold. We

will make thee borders of gold with studs of silver. While the king sitteth at his table, my spikenard sendeth forth the smell thereof. A bundle of myrrh is my well-beloved unto me; he shall lie all night betwixt my breasts. My beloved is unto me as a cluster of camphire in the vineyards of Engedi. Behold, thou art fair, my love; behold, thou art fair; thou hast doves' eyes. Behold, thou art fair, my beloved, yea, pleasant: also our bed is green. The beams of our house are cedar, and our rafters of fir.

Song of Solomon 1:7-17

2443. Regarding the ways of God, there's a *method to the Genius*. If you pay attention, you may learn a thing or two.

O the depth of the riches both of the wisdom and knowledge of God! How unsearchable are his judgments, and his ways past finding out! For who hath known the mind of the Lord? Or who hath been his counsellor? Or who hath first given to him, and it shall be recompensed unto him again? For of him, and through him, and to him, are all things: to whom be glory for ever. Amen.

Romans 11:33-36

2444. You were made to live happy for a lifetime. Therefore, no single day is the *"end of the world."* Cheer up! It will look better in the morning.

For his anger endureth but a moment; in his favour is life: weeping may endure for a night, but joy cometh in the morning.

Psalm 30:5

2445. Miracles don't make believers. Some things only come by discernment.

Jesus answered and said unto her, if thou knewest the gift of God, and who it is that saith to thee, give me to drink; thou wouldest have asked of him, and he would have given thee living water.

John 4:10

2446. Attitude determines altitude. Therefore, keep soaring like an eagle!

But they that wait upon the Lord shall renew their strength; they shall mount up with wings as eagles; they shall run, and not be weary; and they shall walk, and not faint.

Isaiah 40:31

2447. Faith is a *free-for-all*!

The sower soweth the word. And these are they by the way side, where the word is sown; but when they have heard, Satan cometh immediately, and taketh away the word that was sown in their hearts. And these are they likewise which are sown on stony ground; who, when they have heard the word,

immediately receive it with gladness; And have no root in themselves, and so endure but for a time: afterward, when affliction or persecution ariseth for the word's sake, immediately they are offended. And these are they, which are sown among thorns; such as hear the word, And the cares of this world, and the deceitfulness of riches, and the lusts of other things entering in, choke the word, and it becometh unfruitful. And these are they which are sown on good ground; such as hear the word, and receive it, and bring forth fruit, some thirtyfold, some sixty, and some an hundred.

Mark 4:14-20

2448. God is causing success and wealth to accrue to your life account, due to your continual, diligent efforts of excellence. It is as sure as compound interest accrues to your investments in a savings or retirement account. Just continue to make direct deposits into life through your daily living and giving.

He that diligently seeketh good procureth favour . . .

Proverbs 11:27a

2449. Regarding how to accomplish your destiny, a turtle with a map will get there faster than a jack rabbit cutting his or her own *bunny trail*.

Without counsel purposes are disappointed: but in the multitude of counsellors they are established.

Proverbs 15:2

2450. The areas where we lack perfect performance create a space for God's grace to enter in and make up the difference. Often we wouldn't pay attention to His intimate involvement in our lives, if He didn't allow times that revealed our weaknesses.

For this thing I besought the Lord thrice that it might depart from me. And he said unto me, my grace is sufficient for thee: for my strength is made perfect in weakness. Most gladly therefore will I rather glory in my infirmities, that the power of Christ may rest upon me.

2 Corinthians 12:8-9

2451. Regarding the benefits of marriage, husbands and wives signed up for the *lifetime package.*

And he answered and said unto them, have ye not read, that he which made them at the beginning made them male and female, and said, for this cause shall a man leave father and mother, and shall cleave to his wife: and they twain shall be one flesh? Wherefore they are no more twain, but one flesh. What therefore God hath joined together, let not man put asunder.

Matthew 19:4-6

2452. We don't always need a sign, as we walk by faith and not by sight. However, it's always a beautiful thing to receive one!

I do set my bow in the cloud, and it shall be for a token of a covenant between me and the earth. And it shall come to pass, when I bring a cloud over the earth, that the bow shall be seen in the cloud: and I will remember my covenant, which is between me and you and every living creature of all flesh; and the waters shall no more become a flood to destroy all flesh. And the bow shall be in the cloud; and I will look upon it, that I may remember the everlasting covenant between God and every living creature of all flesh that is upon the earth. And God said unto Noah, this is the token of the covenant, which I have established between me and all flesh that is upon the earth.

Genesis 9:13-17

2453. Regarding how to accomplish your dreams, here are the three phases of a dream: It's possible. It's probable. It's proven.

Now therefore perform the doing of it; that as there was a readiness to will, so there may be a performance also out of that which ye have. For if there be first a willing mind, it is accepted according to that a man hath, and not according to that he hath not.

2 Corinthians 8:11-12

2454. Thank God for a strong mother who knows how to say "No!" A strong mother will teach you how to be strong.

And the king of Egypt spake to the Hebrew midwives, of which the name of the one was Shiphrah, and the name of the other Puah: And he said, when ye do the office of a midwife to the Hebrew women, and see them upon the stools; if it be a son, then ye shall kill him: but if it be a daughter, then she shall live. But the midwives feared God, and did not as the king of Egypt commanded them, but saved the men children alive. And the king of Egypt called for the midwives, and said unto them, why have ye done this thing, and have saved the men children alive? And the midwives said unto pharaoh, because the Hebrew women are not as the Egyptian women; for they are lively, and are delivered ere the midwives come in unto them. Therefore God dealt well with the midwives: and the people multiplied, and waxed very mighty. And it came to pass, because the midwives feared God, that he made them houses.

Exodus 1:15-21

2455. Everything in your life emanates from your premise. If you have a premise of victory, worthiness, inheritance, birthright, preeminence, authority, and ownership, then, you can never truly be defeated or become anyone else's slave or subservient. Everything in your life emanates from having the proper premise.

I have said, ye are gods; and all of you are children of the Most High.

Psalm 82:6

2456. What you're doing today is a down payment on your future.

And as she was going to fetch it, he called to her, and said, bring me, I pray thee, a morsel of bread in thine hand. And she said, as the Lord thy God liveth, I have not a cake, but an handful of meal in a barrel, and a little oil in a cruse: and, behold, I am gathering two sticks, that I may go in and dress it for me and my son, that we may eat it, and die. And Elijah said unto her, fear not; go and do as thou hast said: but make me thereof a little cake first, and bring it unto me, and after make for thee and for thy son. For thus saith the Lord God of Israel, the barrel of meal shall not waste, neither shall the cruse of oil fail, until the day that the Lord sendeth rain upon the earth. And she went and did according to the saying of Elijah: and she, and he, and her house, did eat many days.

1 Kings 17:11-15

2457. Regarding borrowing and credit, if you don't have the money to pay for it right out, you don't have the money to get into debt for it. Debt should be a tool you control, rather than a slave-master that controls you.

The rich ruleth over the poor, and the borrower is servant to the lender.

Proverbs 22:7

2458. Regarding friendship, if you can't be honest, and you can't be free, then, that is a sign that that friendship hasn't developed to where it should be.

Open rebuke is better than secret love. Faithful are the wounds of a friend; but the kisses of an enemy are deceitful.

Proverbs 27:5-6

2459. Despise not the intelligent soul who seems slow and plodding, because he or she just might be *plotting* a great success.

For they got not the land in possession by their own sword, neither did their own arm save them: but thy right hand, and thine arm, and the light of thy countenance, because thou hadst a favour unto them.

Psalm 44:3

2460. Even people who don't notice God, God notices them. God will reward every person, according to his or her works.

But he that doeth wrong shall receive for the wrong, which he hath done: and there is no respect of persons.

Colossians 3:25

2461. If you know that your best years were not behind you, then, you can be certain that your best years must be

ahead of you. Therefore, be thankful for your past, but keep striving for your future!

Brethren, I count not myself to have apprehended: but this one thing I do, forgetting those things which are behind, and reaching forth unto those things which are before, I press toward the mark for the prize of the high calling of God in Christ Jesus.

Philippians 3:13-14

2462. Most movements that require a *bandwagon* are usually going in the wrong direction.

Now Korah, the son of Izhar, the son of Kohath, the son of Levi, and Dathan and Abiram, the sons of Eliab, and on, the son of Peleth, sons of Reuben, took men: And they rose up before Moses, with certain of the children of Israel, two hundred and fifty princes of the assembly, famous in the congregation, men of renown: And they gathered themselves together against Moses and against Aaron, and said unto them, ye take too much upon you, seeing all the congregation are holy, every one of them, and the Lord is among them: wherefore then lift ye up yourselves above the congregation of the Lord? And when Moses heard it, he fell upon his face: And he spake unto Korah and unto all his company, saying, even to morrow the Lord will shew who are his, and who is holy; and will cause him to come near unto him: even him whom he hath chosen will he cause to come near unto him. This do; take you censers, Korah, and all his company; And put fire therein, and put incense in them before the Lord to

morrow: and it shall be that the man whom the Lord doth choose, he shall be holy: ye take too much upon you, ye sons of Levi. And Moses said unto Korah, hear, I pray you, ye sons of Levi: Seemeth it but a small thing unto you, that the God of Israel hath separated you from the congregation of Israel, to bring you near to himself to do the service of the tabernacle of the Lord, and to stand before the congregation to minister unto them? And he hath brought thee near to him, and all thy brethren the sons of Levi with thee: and seek ye the priesthood also? For which cause both thou and all thy company are gathered together against the Lord: and what is Aaron, that ye murmur against him? And Moses sent to call Dathan and Abiram, the sons of Eliab: which said, we will not come up: Is it a small thing that thou hast brought us up out of a land that floweth with milk and honey, to kill us in the wilderness, except thou make thyself altogether a prince over us? Moreover thou hast not brought us into a land that floweth with milk and honey, or given us inheritance of fields and vineyards: wilt thou put out the eyes of these men? We will not come up. And Moses was very wroth, and said unto the Lord, respect not thou their offering: I have not taken one ass from them, neither have I hurt one of them. And Moses said unto Korah, be thou and all thy company before the Lord, thou, and they, and Aaron, to morrow: And take every man his censer, and put incense in them, and bring ye before the Lord every man his censer, two hundred and fifty censers; thou also, and Aaron, each of you his censer. And they took every man his censer, and put fire in them, and laid incense thereon, and stood in the door of the tabernacle of the congregation with Moses and Aaron. And Korah gathered all the congregation against them unto the door of the tabernacle

of the congregation: and the glory of the Lord appeared unto all the congregation. And the Lord spake unto Moses and unto Aaron, saying, Separate yourselves from among this congregation, that I may consume them in a moment. And they fell upon their faces, and said, O God, the God of the spirits of all flesh, shall one man sin, and wilt thou be wroth with all the congregation? And the Lord spake unto Moses, saying, Speak unto the congregation, saying, get you up from about the tabernacle of Korah, Dathan, and Abiram. And Moses rose up and went unto Dathan and Abiram; and the elders of Israel followed him. And he spake unto the congregation, saying, depart, I pray you, from the tents of these wicked men, and touch nothing of their's, lest ye be consumed in all their sins. So they gat up from the tabernacle of Korah, Dathan, and Abiram, on every side: and Dathan and Abiram came out, and stood in the door of their tents, and their wives, and their sons, and their little children. And Moses said, hereby ye shall know that the Lord hath sent me to do all these works; for I have not done them of mine own mind. If these men die the common death of all men, or if they be visited after the visitation of all men; then the Lord hath not sent me. But if the Lord make a new thing, and the earth open her mouth, and swallow them up, with all that appertain unto them, and they go down quick into the pit; then ye shall understand that these men have provoked the Lord. And it came to pass, as he had made an end of speaking all these words, that the ground clave asunder that was under them: And the earth opened her mouth, and swallowed them up, and their houses, and all the men that appertained unto Korah, and all their goods. They, and all that appertained to them, went down alive into the pit, and the

earth closed upon them: and they perished from among the congregation. And all Israel that were round about them fled at the cry of them: for they said, lest the earth swallow us up also. And there came out a fire from the Lord, and consumed the two hundred and fifty men that offered incense. And the Lord spake unto Moses, saying, Speak unto Eleazar the son of Aaron the priest, that he take up the censers out of the burning, and scatter thou the fire yonder; for they are hallowed. The censers of these sinners against their own souls, let them make them broad plates for a covering of the altar: for they offered them before the Lord, therefore they are hallowed: and they shall be a sign unto the children of Israel. And Eleazar the priest took the brasen censers, wherewith they that were burnt had offered; and they were made broad plates for a covering of the altar: To be a memorial unto the children of Israel, that no stranger, which is not of the seed of Aaron, come near to offer incense before the Lord; that he be not as Korah, and as his company: as the Lord said to him by the hand of Moses.

Numbers 16:1-40

2463. After you've dealt with *"the end of the world!"* a few times in your life, you learn to realize that tomorrow always comes.

There hath no temptation taken you but such as is common to man: but God is faithful, who will not suffer you to be tempted above that ye are able; but will with the temptation also make a way to escape, that ye may be able to bear it.

1 Corinthians 10:13

2464. *"Men are from Mars/Women are from Venus"*, and, you have been assigned to work out your differences together on Earth in the God ordained relationship called marriage.

Likewise, ye husbands, dwell with them according to knowledge, giving honour unto the wife, as unto the weaker vessel, and as being heirs together of the grace of life; that your prayers be not hindered.

1 Peter 3:7

2465. Don't say everything that you think. Do *think* everything that you say.

The heart of the righteous studieth to answer: but the mouth of the wicked poureth out evil things.

Proverbs 15:28

2466. Confess your faith resolutely. Demonstrate your faith undeniably. Thereby, you may turn your critics into believers. Thus, they will have the opportunity to believe in the God of your faith through your demonstration of your faith.

Yea, a man may say, thou hast faith, and I have works: shew me thy faith without thy works, and I will shew thee my faith by my works.

James 2:18

2467. Regarding success, if you do your part to work together with God, then, everything will work together for your good.

But Jesus answered them, my father worketh hitherto, and I work.

John 5:17

2468. Some people say "What a difference a day makes!" However, I say "What a difference a *prayer* makes!" If you want a brighter day, then, pray.

And when thou prayest, thou shalt not be as the hypocrites are: for they love to pray standing in the synagogues and in the corners of the streets, that they may be seen of men. Verily I say unto you, they have their reward. But thou, when thou prayest, enter into thy closet, and when thou hast shut thy door, pray to thy father which is in secret; and thy father which seeth in secret shall reward thee openly.

Matthew 6:5-6

2469. You are one with the *Rock of Wisdom* through whom all of civilization was established. You are God's direct offspring. He is your Heavenly Father. There is no answer that is out of your reach. You have the mind of the "Architect and Engineer" of all productive things. You are a son or daughter of God. Therefore, live in your birthright to reign in life today as a king or queen, and continue to exercise your

Pastor Terrance Levise Turner, MBA

God-given authority on Earth. You are a part of the *Eternal Living Stone*!

Hear; for I will speak of excellent things; and the opening of my lips shall be right things. For my mouth shall speak truth; and wickedness is an abomination to my lips. All the words of my mouth are in righteousness; there is nothing froward or perverse in them. They are all plain to him that understandeth, and right to them that find knowledge. Receive my instruction, and not silver; and knowledge rather than choice gold. For wisdom is better than rubies; and all the things that may be desired are not to be compared to it. I wisdom dwell with prudence, and find out knowledge of witty inventions. The fear of the Lord is to hate evil: pride, and arrogancy, and the evil way, and the froward mouth, do I hate. Counsel is mine, and sound wisdom: I am understanding; I have strength. By me kings reign, and princes decree justice. By me princes rule, and nobles, even all the judges of the earth. I love them that love me; and those that seek me early shall find me. Riches and honour are with me; yea, durable riches and righteousness. My fruit is better than gold, yea, than fine gold; and my revenue than choice silver. I lead in the way of righteousness, in the midst of the paths of judgment: That I may cause those that love me to inherit substance; and I will fill their treasures. The Lord possessed me in the beginning of his way, before his works of old. I was set up from everlasting, from the beginning, or ever the earth was. When there were no depths, I was brought forth; when there were no fountains abounding with water. Before the mountains were settled, before the hills was I brought forth: While as yet he had not made the earth, nor the fields, nor the

highest part of the dust of the world. When he prepared the heavens, I was there: when he set a compass upon the face of the depth: When he established the clouds above: when he strengthened the fountains of the deep: When he gave to the sea his decree, that the waters should not pass his commandment: when he appointed the foundations of the earth: Then I was by him, as one brought up with him: and I was daily his delight, rejoicing always before him; Rejoicing in the habitable part of his earth; and my delights were with the sons of men. Now therefore hearken unto me, O ye children: for blessed are they that keep my ways. Hear instruction, and be wise, and refuse it not. Blessed is the man that heareth me, watching daily at my gates, waiting at the posts of my doors. For whoso findeth me findeth life, and shall obtain favour of the Lord.

Proverbs 8:6-35

2470. Some devils can't be cast out. They must be *taught* out. You can't have a crazy devil, if you have a *sane* mind. It takes the teaching of God's anointed Word to drive some devils out. A crazy devil can't be comfortable in a mind that becomes renewed with the light of God's Word. Your true deliverance is in God's Word!

That ye put off concerning the former conversation the old man, which is corrupt according to the deceitful lusts; and be renewed in the spirit of your mind; and that ye put on the new man, which after God is created in righteousness and true holiness. Wherefore putting away lying, speak every man truth with his neighbour: for we are members one of another.

Be ye angry, and sin not: let not the sun go down upon your wrath: neither give place to the devil.

Ephesians 4:22-27

2471. If you woke up this morning in your right mind, and could find a *pair of matching socks*, then, that surely is a sign that it's going to be a good day! In all things give thanks!

Rejoice evermore. Pray without ceasing. In every thing give thanks: for this is the will of God in Christ Jesus concerning you.

1 Thessalonians 5:16-18

2472. Never talk about your problems with people who can't solve them. Jesus is on the *main line*. Tell Him what you want!

Rejoice in the Lord alway: and again I say, rejoice. Let your moderation be known unto all men. The Lord is at hand. Be careful for nothing; but in every thing by prayer and supplication with thanksgiving let your requests be made known unto God. And the peace of God, which passeth all understanding, shall keep your hearts and minds through Christ Jesus. Finally, brethren, whatsoever things are true, whatsoever things are honest, whatsoever things are just, whatsoever things are pure, whatsoever things are lovely, whatsoever things are of good report; if there be any virtue, and if there be any praise, think on these things. Those things,

which ye have both learned, and received, and heard, and seen in me, do: and the God of peace shall be with you.

Philippians 4:4-9

2473. Regarding your pursuit of success, you might not be certain, but keep working. And, the more you keep working, the more certain you will become.

Even so faith, if it hath not works, is dead, being alone. Yea, a man may say, thou hast faith, and I have works: shew me thy faith without thy works, and I will shew thee my faith by my works.

James 2:17-18

2474. Education, training, skill, and natural talent are the keys to extraordinary success! All you have to do is to put them to work for you!

For the kingdom of heaven is as a man travelling into a far country, who called his own servants, and delivered unto them his goods. And unto one he gave five talents, to another two, and to another one; to every man according to his several ability; and straightway took his journey. Then he that had received the five talents went and traded with the same, and made them other five talents. And likewise he that had received two, he also gained other two. But he that had received one went and digged in the earth, and hid his Lord's money. After a long time the Lord of those servants cometh, and reckoneth with them. And so he that had received five

talents came and brought other five talents, saying, Lord, thou deliveredst unto me five talents: behold, I have gained beside them five talents more. His Lord said unto him, well done, thou good and faithful servant: thou hast been faithful over a few things, I will make thee ruler over many things: enter thou into the joy of thy Lord. He also that had received two talents came and said, Lord, thou deliveredst unto me two talents: behold, I have gained two other talents beside them. His Lord said unto him, well done, good and faithful servant; thou hast been faithful over a few things, I will make thee ruler over many things: enter thou into the joy of thy Lord. Then he which had received the one talent came and said, Lord, I knew thee that thou art an hard man, reaping where thou hast not sown, and gathering where thou hast not strawed: And I was afraid, and went and hid thy talent in the earth: lo, there thou hast that is thine. His Lord answered and said unto him, thou wicked and slothful servant, thou knewest that I reap where I sowed not, and gather where I have not strawed: Thou oughtest therefore to have put my money to the exchangers, and then at my coming I should have received mine own with usury. Take therefore the talent from him, and give it unto him, which hath ten talents. For unto every one that hath shall be given, and he shall have abundance: but from him that hath not shall be taken away even that which he hath.

Matthew 25:14-29

2475. Regarding the difference between wisdom and religion: Religion pacifies. Wisdom empowers. Religion helps you to *get along*. Wisdom helps you to *get out*. Religion helps

you to endure. Wisdom helps to effect change. Religion helps you to suffer long. Wisdom empowers you to redeem the time. Religion legitimizes your lack of progress. Wisdom *demands* that you succeed. Religion comforts your complacency. Wisdom demands that you *"Get 'er done!"* Religion helps you to be content to walk around the mountain for 40 years. Wisdom demands and gives the plan for you to possess the land.

Even so faith, if it hath not works, is dead, being alone. Yea, a man may say, thou hast faith, and I have works: shew me thy faith without thy works, and I will shew thee my faith by my works.

James 2:17-18

2478. Religion and envy attempts to minimize and marginalize the value of the vessel containing extraordinary gifts. Religion and envy often esteems the gift that is poured out, without esteeming the vessel containing the gift. However, Jesus esteemed Himself as *the gift*, and He esteemed the gift that He came to give. The person of His body was a gift to be reverenced, as well as the gift that He gave in the outpouring of His precious blood for our salvation.

Jesus answered and said unto her, if thou knewest the gift of God, and who it is that saith to thee, give me to drink; thou wouldest have asked of him, and he would have given thee living water.

John 4:10

2479. When faced with the decision of something that could be advantageous, yet you have limited knowledge of it, then, you have to *step out* to find out. In many cases, the only way to truly find out is to *step out*. Do research to find out as much as possible before hand. When you step out, then, you will find out. Many times, you'll find out that you've found something very special!

And Jonathan said to the young man that bare his armour, come, and let us go over unto the garrison of these uncircumcised: it may be that the Lord will work for us: for there is no restraint to the Lord to save by many or by few.

1 Samuel 14:6

2480. You can't turn your eyes away from excellence when you see it and experience it, because it's rarely seen.

Seest thou a man diligent in his business? He shall stand before kings; he shall not stand before mean men.

Proverbs 22:29

2481. If you want to be *"blessed indeed"*, then, do the *work* indeed, and, then, you will be blessed indeed.

And Jabez was more honourable than his brethren: and his mother called his name Jabez, saying, because I bare him with sorrow. And Jabez called on the God of Israel, saying, Oh that thou wouldest bless me indeed, and enlarge my coast, and that thine hand might be with me, and that thou wouldest keep me

from evil, that it may not grieve me! And God granted him that which he requested.

1 Chronicles 4:9-10

2482. If everyone you came in contact with today seemed to be a problem to you, and you were not able to change them; but, rather, you gave up and just chose to focus on changing you; and, suddenly, the problems decreased, then, you were the one with the problem.

He that is slow to anger is better than the mighty; and he that ruleth his spirit than he that taketh a city.

Proverbs 16:32

2483. You're on the winning team if you're on the side of righteousness. The side of righteousness is the winning side. And, if God be for you, who can be against you? You're on the winning team!

What shall we then say to these things? If God be for us, who can be against us?

Romans 8:31

2484. Take time to bend your knees in prayer to your Heavenly Father, in Jesus name. When you stand back up you will be able to walk straighter.

And when thou prayest, thou shalt not be as the hypocrites are: for they love to pray standing in the synagogues and in

the corners of the streets, that they may be seen of men. Verily I say unto you, they have their reward. But thou, when thou prayest, enter into thy closet, and when thou hast shut thy door, pray to thy father which is in secret; and thy father which seeth in secret shall reward thee openly.

Matthew 6:5-6

2485. Regarding criticism, why listen to a *zero*, when you know that you are a *hero*?

And it came to pass, that when Jesus had finished these parables, he departed thence. And when he was come into his own country, he taught them in their synagogue, insomuch that they were astonished, and said, whence hath this man this wisdom, and these mighty works? Is not this the carpenter's son? Is not his mother called Mary? And his brethren, James, and Joses, and Simon, and Judas? And his sisters, are they not all with us? Whence then hath this man all these things? And they were offended in him. But Jesus said unto them, a prophet is not without honour, save in his own country, and in his own house. And he did not many mighty works there because of their unbelief.

Matthew 13:53-58

2486. If you obeyed God, and stepped out in faith, yet, you didn't see the expected victory immediately, then, don't be disheartened. It was still a victory. It was a *spiritual* victory to overcome the atmosphere of your problem or opposition. Sometimes, the first step of a victory is unseen to the natural

eye. All we have to do is to obey God. And, eventually every wall of opposition will come *crumbling down!*

Now Jericho was straitly shut up because of the children of Israel: none went out, and none came in. And the Lord said unto Joshua, see, I have given into thine hand Jericho, and the king thereof, and the mighty men of valour. And ye shall compass the city, all ye men of war, and go round about the city once. Thus shalt thou do six days. And seven priests shall bear before the ark seven trumpets of rams' horns: and the seventh day ye shall compass the city seven times, and the priests shall blow with the trumpets. And it shall come to pass, that when they make a long blast with the ram's horn, and when ye hear the sound of the trumpet, all the people shall shout with a great shout; and the wall of the city shall fall down flat, and the people shall ascend up every man straight before him. And Joshua the son of Nun called the priests, and said unto them, take up the ark of the covenant, and let seven priests bear seven trumpets of rams' horns before the ark of the Lord. And he said unto the people, pass on, and compass the city, and let him that is armed pass on before the ark of the Lord. And it came to pass, when Joshua had spoken unto the people, that the seven priests bearing the seven trumpets of rams' horns passed on before the Lord, and blew with the trumpets: and the ark of the covenant of the Lord followed them. And the armed men went before the priests that blew with the trumpets, and the rereward came after the ark, the priests going on, and blowing with the trumpets. And Joshua had commanded the people, saying, ye shall not shout, nor make any noise with your voice, neither shall any word proceed out of your mouth, until the day I bid you shout; then

shall ye shout. So the ark of the Lord compassed the city, going about it once: and they came into the camp, and lodged in the camp. And Joshua rose early in the morning, and the priests took up the ark of the Lord. And seven priests bearing seven trumpets of rams' horns before the ark of the Lord went on continually, and blew with the trumpets: and the armed men went before them; but the rereward came after the ark of the Lord, the priests going on, and blowing with the trumpets. And the second day they compassed the city once, and returned into the camp: so they did six days. And it came to pass on the seventh day, that they rose early about the dawning of the day, and compassed the city after the same manner seven times: only on that day they compassed the city seven times. And it came to pass at the seventh time, when the priests blew with the trumpets, Joshua said unto the people, shout; for the Lord hath given you the city. And the city shall be accursed, even it, and all that are therein, to the Lord: only Rahab the harlot shall live, she and all that are with her in the house, because she hid the messengers that we sent. And ye, in any wise keep yourselves from the accursed thing, lest ye make yourselves accursed, when ye take of the accursed thing, and make the camp of Israel a curse, and trouble it. But all the silver, and gold, and vessels of brass and iron, are consecrated unto the Lord: they shall come into the treasury of the Lord. So the people shouted when the priests blew with the trumpets: and it came to pass, when the people heard the sound of the trumpet, and the people shouted with a great shout, that the wall fell down flat, so that the people went up into the city, every man straight before him, and they took the city.

Distinguished Wisdom Presents... "Living Proverbs"–Vol.5

Joshua 6:1-20

2487. Refine your gifts and talents. Turn them into skills. Get your education. Put forth effort. And, you will guarantee a profitable result.

Seest thou a man diligent in his business? He shall stand before kings; he shall not stand before mean men.

Proverbs 22:29

2488. Regarding opportunities, as long as you stay *hungry*, God will keep feeding you with new opportunities. However, if you stop being hungry, the opportunities will dry up. God doesn't waste opportunities on people who are not hungry enough to seize them! Stay *hungry*!

For the kingdom of heaven is as a man travelling into a far country, who called his own servants, and delivered unto them his goods. And unto one he gave five talents, to another two, and to another one; to every man according to his several ability; and straightway took his journey. Then he that had received the five talents went and traded with the same, and made them other five talents. And likewise he that had received two, he also gained other two. But he that had received one went and digged in the earth, and hid his Lord's money. After a long time the Lord of those servants cometh, and reckoneth with them. And so he that had received five talents came and brought other five talents, saying, Lord, thou deliveredst unto me five talents: behold, I have gained beside them five talents more. His Lord said unto him, well done,

thou good and faithful servant: thou hast been faithful over a few things, I will make thee ruler over many things: enter thou into the joy of thy Lord. He also that had received two talents came and said, Lord, thou deliveredst unto me two talents: behold, I have gained two other talents beside them. His Lord said unto him, well done, good and faithful servant; thou hast been faithful over a few things, I will make thee ruler over many things: enter thou into the joy of thy Lord. Then he which had received the one talent came and said, Lord, I knew thee that thou art an hard man, reaping where thou hast not sown, and gathering where thou hast not strawed: and I was afraid, and went and hid thy talent in the earth: lo, there thou hast that is thine. His Lord answered and said unto him, thou wicked and slothful servant, thou knewest that I reap where I sowed not, and gather where I have not strawed: thou oughtest therefore to have put my money to the exchangers, and then at my coming I should have received mine own with usury. Take therefore the talent from him, and give it unto him, which hath ten talents. For unto every one that hath shall be given, and he shall have abundance: but from him that hath not shall be taken away even that which he hath.

Matthew 25:14-29

2489. No human truly has room to criticize or condemn. We really only have room to empathize.

Brethren, if a man be overtaken in a fault, ye which are spiritual, restore such an one in the spirit of meekness; considering thyself, lest thou also be tempted.

Galatians 6:1

2490. If the spotlight of scrutiny shines upon you, then, show that you're a *star*!

But ye are a chosen generation, a royal priesthood, an holy nation, a peculiar people; that ye should shew forth the praises of him who hath called you out of darkness into his marvellous light.

1 Peter 2:9

2491. Cheer up! God loves you!

I will praise thee; for I am fearfully and wonderfully made: marvellous are thy works; and that my soul knoweth right well.

Psalm 139:14

2492. Regarding releasing your potential, one *diamond* from your mind can enrich your life for a lifetime.

He that tilleth his land shall be satisfied with bread: but he that followeth vain persons is void of understanding.

Proverbs 12:11

2493. Regarding how to become rich? 1) Become *enriched* by investing in education, spiritual development, and adherence to moral values. 2) Create riches, by transforming your values into tangible products and services. 3) Promote

what you have produced and become to those that need it, and who are willing and able to compensate you for it. That's how you become rich!

But his delight is in the law of the Lord; and in his law doth he meditate day and night. And he shall be like a tree planted by the rivers of water, that bringeth forth his fruit in his season; his leaf also shall not wither; and whatsoever he doeth shall prosper.

Psalm 1:2-3

2494. The way to overcome fear and to have prosperity and peace in your experience on Earth is to love the Lord your God with all your heart, with all your soul, and with all your strength; and, to love yourself with all your heart, with all your soul, and with all your strength; and, to love your neighbor as you love yourself.

Jesus said unto him, thou shalt love the Lord thy God with all thy heart, and with all thy soul, and with all thy mind. This is the first and great commandment. And the second is like unto it, thou shalt love thy neighbour as thyself. On these two commandments hang all the law and the prophets.

Matthew 22:37-40

2495. We are the "Greater Works Generation." But, you've got to believe it in order to achieve it!

Verily, verily, I say unto you, he that believeth on me, the works that I do shall he do also; and greater works than these shall he do; because I go unto my father.

John 14:12

2496. You must *think* rich, before you can be rich. You must *know* that you're rich, before you can grow rich. Riches start with a state of mind.

For as he thinketh in his heart, so is he...

Proverbs 23:7a

2497. The key to long-term success is to work smart. Not hard. You must budget your mental energy. You must budget your physical energy. You must budget your spiritual energy. You must budget your financial resources. You must budget your dreams. And, you must budget your time. Work smart. Not hard. It's the key to long-term success.

There be four things which are little upon the earth, but they are exceeding wise: The ants are a people not strong, yet they prepare their meat in the summer; The conies are but a feeble folk, yet make they their houses in the rocks; The locusts have no king, yet go they forth all of them by bands; The spider taketh hold with her hands, and is in kings' palaces.

Proverbs 30:24-28

2498. In life, you have to do what you can do. You must know that you're not working alone. Don't doubt your effectiveness. Rather, be assured that you will successful, because you're working along with God.

But Jesus answered them, my father worketh hitherto, and I work.

John 5:17

2499. God gives us daily grace to totally fulfill our race.

Thy shoes shall be iron and brass; and as thy days, so shall thy strength be.

Deuteronomy 33:25

2500. Noah was a *"prosperity preacher"*. And, his message was responsible for saving humanity; at least all of those that listened to and obeyed his message.

And he called his name Noah, saying, this same shall comfort us concerning our work and toil of our hands, because of the ground which the Lord hath cursed.

Genesis 5:29

2501. There's more in store and there is an open door!

For a great door and effectual is opened unto me, and there are many adversaries.

Distinguished Wisdom Presents . . . "Living Proverbs"–Vol.5

1 Corinthians 16:9

2502. Flesh fighting flesh, equals a mess. Be not overcome of evil, but overcome evil with good.

For though we walk in the flesh, we do not war after the flesh: (for the weapons of our warfare are not carnal, but mighty through God to the pulling down of strong holds;) casting down imaginations, and every high thing that exalteth itself against the knowledge of God, and bringing into captivity every thought to the obedience of Christ.

2 Corinthians 10:3-5

2503. Keep on confessing the truth, and it will change any contrary facts.

As it is written, I have made thee a father of many nations,) before him whom he believed, even God, who quickeneth the dead, and calleth those things which be not as though they were. Who against hope believed in hope, that he might become the father of many nations, according to that which was spoken, so shall thy seed be. And being not weak in faith, he considered not his own body now dead, when he was about an hundred years old, neither yet the deadness of Sarah's womb: He staggered not at the promise of God through unbelief; but was strong in faith, giving glory to God; and being fully persuaded that, what he had promised, he was able also to perform. And therefore it was imputed to him for righteousness. Now it was not written for his sake alone, that it was imputed to him; but for us also, to whom it shall be

imputed, if we believe on him that raised up Jesus our Lord from the dead; who was delivered for our offences, and was raised again for our justification.

Romans 4:17-25

2504. To become an "overnight success" takes many nights of working *overnight*!

For a dream cometh through the multitude of business; and a fool's voice is known by multitude of words.

Ecclesiastes 5:3

2505. Through *achievement* you become chief. Through *doing* you gain dominion. It's a law that doesn't discriminate. It doesn't matter in what capacity, if you serve better, and if you serve more, you will win.

The hand of the diligent shall bear rule: but the slothful shall be under tribute.

Proverbs 12:24

2506. You must take the necessary steps to be able to open the door when your blessing knocks. You must make the necessary arrangements to be at the train station when your train arrives. You must start out early in the morning to be at the dock when your ship comes in.

In the morning sow thy seed, and in the evening withhold not thine hand: for thou knowest not whether shall prosper, either this or that, or whether they both shall be alike good.

Ecclesiastes 11:6

2507. God's plan is unshakable and unmovable. He has promotion for your life. The best is in the process of happening. You have grace for today and favorable promises for tomorrow.

For all the promises of God in him are yea, and in him amen, unto the glory of God by us.

2 Corinthians 1:20

2508. Sometimes, just your "being" is enough to help somebody. Just shine! Let your light so very much shine before people, so that they will see your good works, and glorify your Heavenly Father.

Ye are the salt of the earth: but if the salt have lost his savour, wherewith shall it be salted? It is thenceforth good for nothing, but to be cast out, and to be trodden under foot of men. Ye are the light of the world. A city that is set on an hill cannot be hid. Neither do men light a candle, and put it under a bushel, but on a candlestick; and it giveth light unto all that are in the house. Let your light so shine before men, that they may see your good works, and glorify your father, which is in heaven.

Matthew 5:13-16

2509. Give up being a supplicant of another's favor. Rather, do what's necessary to make your *own* favor.

He that diligently seeketh good procureth favour: but he that seeketh mischief, it shall come unto him.

Proverbs 11:27

2510. May God reward you for your righteous lifestyle before Him. May He lavishly recompense you for your labor of love. In Jesus name, amen.

For God is not unrighteous to forget your work and labour of love, which ye have shewed toward his name, in that ye have ministered to the saints, and do minister. And we desire that every one of you do shew the same diligence to the full assurance of hope unto the end: that ye be not slothful, but followers of them who through faith and patience inherit the promises.

Hebrews 6:10-12

2511. When your will is rolling in cooperation with God's will, then, nothing can stop you from arriving at your destination.

The appearance of the wheels and their work was like unto the colour of a beryl: and they four had one likeness: and their appearance and their work was as it were a wheel in the middle of a wheel.

Ezekiel 1:16

2512. Regarding discretion, nothing can be said about not saying too much.

The heart of the righteous studieth to answer: but the mouth of the wicked poureth out evil things.

Proverbs 15:28

2513. On Christ the Solid Rock I stand. All other ground is sinking sand. Salvation through faith in the precious blood of Jesus, which was shed on the cross to pay for our sins, is the only blessed assurance we have when all else fails. Whosoever calls upon the name of the Lord, shall be saved. Call on Him today. Say, "Jesus, come into my heart. Be my Lord and Savior. I repent of my sins. I accept you as Lord. Thank you Jesus. I am saved. Amen."

But what saith it? The word is nigh thee, even in thy mouth, and in thy heart: that is, the word of faith, which we preach; that if thou shalt confess with thy mouth the Lord Jesus, and shalt believe in thine heart that God hath raised him from the dead, thou shalt be saved. For with the heart man believeth unto righteousness; and with the mouth confession is made unto salvation. For the scripture saith, whosoever believeth on him shall not be ashamed. For there is no difference between the Jew and the Greek: for the same Lord over all is rich unto all that call upon him. For whosoever shall call upon the name of the Lord shall be saved.

Romans 10:8-13

2514. Here is marriage advice to any new couple: Commit to one another, commit to God, and, commit to a *dream*. That is the key to a successful, long lasting marriage. Your level of *commitment* will determine the level of success in your marriage.

Through wisdom is an house builded; and by understanding it is established: and by knowledge shall the chambers be filled with all precious and pleasant riches.

Proverbs 24:3-4

2515. Always love yourself, because you're your very best friend.

So ought men to love their wives as their own bodies. He that loveth his wife loveth himself. For no man ever yet hated his own flesh; but nourisheth and cherisheth it, even as the Lord the church.

Ephesians 5:28-29

2516. Regarding eating, always choose healthy. Choose life. Be your very best friend.

So ought men to love their wives as their own bodies. He that loveth his wife loveth himself. For no man ever yet hated his own flesh; but nourisheth and cherisheth it, even as the Lord the church.

Ephesians 5:28-29

2517. Regarding preaching, when you hear from the earth, it sounds like common chatter. When you hear from Heaven, it resonates within you, and you know that you've heard from God.

For the word of God is quick, and powerful, and sharper than any twoedged sword, piercing even to the dividing asunder of soul and spirit, and of the joints and marrow, and is a discerner of the thoughts and intents of the heart. Neither is there any creature that is not manifest in his sight: but all things are naked and opened unto the eyes of him with whom we have to do. Seeing then that we have a great high priest, that is passed into the heavens, Jesus the son of God, let us hold fast our profession. For we have not an high priest which cannot be touched with the feeling of our infirmities; but was in all points tempted like as we are, yet without sin. Let us therefore come boldly unto the throne of grace, that we may obtain mercy, and find grace to help in time of need.

Hebrews 4:12-16

2518. The spiritual counselors of God liberate you to excel. Carnal counselors restrain you into the realm of their limited understanding.

Not for that we have dominion over your faith, but are helpers of your joy: for by faith ye stand.

2 Corinthians 1:24

2519. You are special. Always love yourself like there's only one of you, because there *is* only one of you.

I will praise thee; for I am fearfully and wonderfully made: marvellous are thy works; and that my soul knoweth right well.

Psalm 139:14

2520. Don't beat yourself up over what you perceive to be a big mistake. Life is a continuum. It doesn't end over one point.

There is therefore now no condemnation to them which are in Christ Jesus, who walk not after the flesh, but after the spirit. For the law of the spirit of life in Christ Jesus hath made me free from the law of sin and death. For what the law could not do, in that it was weak through the flesh, God sending his own son in the likeness of sinful flesh, and for sin, condemned sin in the flesh: That the righteousness of the law might be fulfilled in us, who walk not after the flesh, but after the spirit.

Romans 8:1-4

2521. Big is too small to describe God. His understanding is *infinite*!

He telleth the number of the stars; he calleth them all by their names. Great is our Lord, and of great power: his understanding is infinite.

Psalm 147:4-5

2522. There are people who are reputed to be smart; but, if they work for the devil, then, they are dumb.

Then shall he say also unto them on the left hand, depart from me, ye cursed, into everlasting fire, prepared for the devil and his angels.

Matthew 25:41

2523. Four *virtues* versus four *vices*. The winner of which will determine your true victory or failure in life. The battle is anger versus patience, fear versus love, sexual vice versus sanctification unto marriage, and, low self-esteem versus proper pride and dignity. These are the critical four. The ones that you submit to will determine your true victory or failure in life.

He that is slow to anger is better than the mighty; and he that ruleth his spirit than he that taketh a city.

Proverbs 16:32

There is no fear in love; but perfect love casteth out fear: because fear hath torment. He that feareth is not made perfect in love.

1 John 4:18

Nevertheless, to avoid fornication, let every man have his own wife, and let every woman have her own husband.

1 Corinthians 7:2

I will praise thee; for I am fearfully and wonderfully made: marvellous are thy works; and that my soul knoweth right well.

Psalm 139:14

2524. Creativity bypasses the realm of what's currently possible. Just because it hasn't been done, doesn't mean that it can't be done. The idea just hasn't found a mind willing to receive it, believe it, and to act upon it.

And Jesus went forth, and saw a great multitude, and was moved with compassion toward them, and he healed their sick. And when it was evening, his disciples came to him, saying, this is a desert place, and the time is now past; send the multitude away, that they may go into the villages, and buy themselves victuals. But Jesus said unto them, they need not depart; give ye them to eat. And they say unto him, we have here but five loaves, and two fishes. He said, bring them hither to me. And he commanded the multitude to sit down on the grass, and took the five loaves, and the two fishes, and looking up to heaven, he blessed, and brake, and gave the loaves to his disciples, and the disciples to the multitude. And they did all eat, and were filled: and they took up of the fragments that remained twelve baskets full. And they that had eaten were about five thousand men, beside women and children.

Matthew 14:14-21

2525. When a man and a woman come together into the covenant of marriage, a new creature is created. There is a spiritual dynamic where God takes the best of her spirit and the best of his spirit and combines it with the Holy Spirit. The virtues created were never before seen in their singleness. Those spiritual virtues are then transferred into their children and posterity. Thus, God has produced, procured, procreated, and perpetuated a godly seed in the earth.

Yet ye say, wherefore? Because the Lord hath been witness between thee and the wife of thy youth, against whom thou hast dealt treacherously: yet is she thy companion, and the wife of thy covenant. And did not he make one? Yet had he the residue of the spirit. And wherefore one? That he might seek a godly seed. Therefore take heed to your spirit, and let none deal treacherously against the wife of his youth.

Malachi 2:14-15

2526. One of the greatest gifts that God can give you is an assignment. One of the greatest gifts that you can give God is obedience to your assignment.

If ye be willing and obedient, ye shall eat the good of the land.

Isaiah 1:19

2527. Wise people know more than they say. Unwise people say more than they know.

The heart of the righteous studieth to answer: but the mouth of the wicked poureth out evil things.

>Proverbs 15:28

2528. Always pray. Sometimes prayer delivers you *from*, and, other times prayer delivers you *through*. However, prayer always delivers you. Therefore, always pray.

And he spake a parable unto them *to this end*, that men ought always to pray, and not to faint.

>Luke 18:1

2529. In relationships, it's always wise to be courteous and kind to others. Though roads have a tendency to disconnect and to go their separate ways, you never know on the journey of life, when that same road will twist and turn back up again. Therefore, it pays to have been friendly to the person that you may meet on the road again in the future.

Now therefore be not grieved, nor angry with yourselves, that ye sold me hither: for God did send me before you to preserve life. For these two years hath the famine been in the land: and yet there are five years, in the which there shall neither be earing nor harvest. And God sent me before you to preserve you a posterity in the earth, and to save your lives by a great deliverance. So now it was not you that sent me hither, but God: and he hath made me a father to pharaoh, and Lord of all his house, and a ruler throughout all the land of Egypt. Haste ye, and go up to my father, and say unto him, thus saith thy

son Joseph, God hath made me Lord of all Egypt: come down unto me, tarry not: and thou shalt dwell in the land of Goshen, and thou shalt be near unto me, thou, and thy children, and thy children's children, and thy flocks, and thy herds, and all that thou hast: and there will I nourish thee; for yet there are five years of famine; lest thou, and thy household, and all that thou hast, come to poverty.

Genesis 45:5-11

2530. Often, on the journey of life, God allows time and circumstances to happen in your life to separate the *"wheat from the chaff."* He does this so that when you get to where you're destined to be, there won't be a lot of useless things or people *floating around* your destiny.

The prophet that hath a dream, let him tell a dream; and he that hath my word, let him speak my word faithfully. What is the chaff to the wheat? Saith the Lord. Is not my word like as a fire? Saith the Lord; and like a hammer that breaketh the rock in pieces?

Jeremiah 23:28-29

2531. May you always abide on the *"longi"*-side of the latitude of God's mercy.

The Lord is merciful and gracious, slow to anger, and plenteous in mercy. He will not always chide: neither will he keep his anger for ever. He hath not dealt with us after our sins; nor rewarded us according to our iniquities. For as the

Pastor Terrance Levise Turner, MBA

heaven is high above the earth, so great is his mercy toward them that fear him. As far as the east is from the west, so far hath he removed our transgressions from us. Like as a father pitieth his children, so the Lord pitieth them that fear him. For he knoweth our frame; he remembereth that we are dust. As for man, his days are as grass: as a flower of the field, so he flourisheth. For the wind passeth over it, and it is gone; and the place thereof shall know it no more. But the mercy of the Lord is from everlasting to everlasting upon them that fear him, and his righteousness unto children's children; To such as keep his covenant, and to those that remember his commandments to do them.

Psalm 103:8-18

2532. Any good mother eagle wants to see their eaglets soar. Even though the eaglets must leave the nest of origin, and the relationship will never be as dependent as it was before. The good mother eagle knows that her chief responsibility and success is to raise up a new mature eagle that has the ability to spread his or her own wings and soar into the highest places possible for his or her life.

As an eagle stirreth up her nest, fluttereth over her young, spreadeth abroad her wings, taketh them, beareth them on her wings: so the Lord alone did lead him, and there was no strange God with him.

Deuteronomy 32:11-12

2533. Keep seeking the Lord. Those who seek Him shall find Him. Those who have found Him should keep seeking Him.

Seek the Lord and his strength, seek his face continually.

> 1 Chronicles 16:11

2534. In regard to your success, if you keep on stirring the pot and adding the right ingredients, you will eventually have *soup*.

Blessed is every one that feareth the Lord; that walketh in his ways. For thou shalt eat the labour of thine hands: happy shalt thou be, and it shall be well with thee.

> Psalm 128:1

2535. A husband, when he is young, sows the greater amount of his seed from his loins. However, as he grows older he should sow more lasting seed from his mind.

Hear, ye children, the instruction of a father, and attend to know understanding. For I give you good doctrine, forsake ye not my law. For I was my father's son, tender and only beloved in the sight of my mother. He taught me also, and said unto me, let thine heart retain my words: keep my commandments, and live. Get wisdom, get understanding: forget it not; neither decline from the words of my mouth. Forsake her not, and she shall preserve thee: love her, and she shall keep thee. Wisdom is the principal thing; therefore get

wisdom: and with all thy getting get understanding. Exalt her, and she shall promote thee: she shall bring thee to honour, when thou dost embrace her. She shall give to thine head an ornament of grace: a crown of glory shall she deliver to thee. Hear, o my son, and receive my sayings; and the years of thy life shall be many. I have taught thee in the way of wisdom; I have led thee in right paths. When thou goest, thy steps shall not be straitened; and when thou runnest, thou shalt not stumble. Take fast hold of instruction; let her not go: keep her; for she is thy life. Enter not into the path of the wicked, and go not in the way of evil men. Avoid it, pass not by it, turn from it, and pass away. For they sleep not, except they have done mischief; and their sleep is taken away, unless they cause some to fall. For they eat the bread of wickedness, and drink the wine of violence. But the path of the just is as the shining light, that shineth more and more unto the perfect day. The way of the wicked is as darkness: they know not at what they stumble. My son, attend to my words; incline thine ear unto my sayings. Let them not depart from thine eyes; keep them in the midst of thine heart. For they are life unto those that find them, and health to all their flesh. Keep thy heart with all diligence; for out of it are the issues of life. Put away from thee a froward mouth, and perverse lips put far from thee. Let thine eyes look right on, and let thine eyelids look straight before thee. Ponder the path of thy feet, and let all thy ways be established. Turn not to the right hand nor to the left: remove thy foot from evil.

Proverbs 4

2536. Study to do your own business. If you want to win the West, then, you've got to learn *"How The West Was Won?"*

And that ye study to be quiet, and to do your own business, and to work with your own hands, as we commanded you; that ye may walk honestly toward them that are without, and that ye may have lack of nothing.

> 1 Thessalonians 4:11-12

2537. There's always a harvest attached to a seed. It's a natural law as well as a spiritual law. Harvest-time always comes. It's as sure as the Sun rising in the morning, the cold coming in the Winter, the heat coming in the Summer, the flowers blossoming in the Spring, and the crop coming during Harvest. If you have planted the seeds of obedience to God's success principles in His Word, then, you can be assured of a harvest as sure as the Heavens and Earth remain.

While the earth remaineth, seedtime and harvest, and cold and heat, and summer and winter, and day and night shall not cease.

> Genesis 8:22

2538. It doesn't have to be new for it to be true.

Remove not the ancient landmark, which thy fathers have set.

> Proverbs 22:28

2539. The husband is the head of the wife. However, the head is very responsive to the *neck*.

And the Lord God said, it is not good that the man should be alone; I will make him an help meet for him.

Genesis 2:18

2540. Money without morals is meaningless.

Riches profit not in the day of wrath: but righteousness delivereth from death.

Proverbs 11:4

2541. People who allow their envy and insecurities to prompt them to attempt to marginalize or minimize your exceptional gifts, also, minimize the benefit that you were appointed to bring into their lives.

And it came to pass, that when Jesus had finished these parables, he departed thence. And when he was come into his own country, he taught them in their synagogue, insomuch that they were astonished, and said, whence hath this man this wisdom, and these mighty works? Is not this the carpenter's son? Is not his mother called Mary? And his brethren, James, and Joses, and Simon, and Judas? And his sisters, are they not all with us? Whence then hath this man all these things? And they were offended in him. But Jesus said unto them, a prophet is not without honour, save in his own country, and

in his own house. And he did not many mighty works there because of their unbelief.

Matthew 13:53-58

2542. Disrespect is the chief cause of dissolving relationships.

Wherefore the Lord God of Israel saith, I said indeed that thy house, and the house of thy father, should walk before me for ever: but now the Lord saith, be it far from me; for them that honour me I will honour, and they that despise me shall be lightly esteemed.

1 Samuel 2:30

2543. Regarding the *"prosperity gospel"*, true salvation *is* prosperity. That was the first thing that Jesus taught.

The spirit of the Lord is upon me, because he hath anointed me to preach the gospel to the poor; he hath sent me to heal the brokenhearted, to preach deliverance to the captives, and recovering of sight to the blind, to set at liberty them that are bruised, To preach the acceptable year of the Lord.

Luke 4:18-19

2544. Regarding accomplishing your purpose, if you were able to do anything before, then, you can do anything that you need to do now. If you were able to accomplish anything before, or, finish anything (whatever it may be), then, you can

do the other things that you need to do now. If you were able to do anything before, then, you certainly can do anything, *now*.

I can do all things through Christ which strengtheneth me.

Philippians 4:13

2545. The people who are close to you, who truly openly rejoice with you for your success, often, may be far and in between.

And it came to pass, that when Jesus had finished these parables, he departed thence. And when he was come into his own country, he taught them in their synagogue, insomuch that they were astonished, and said, whence hath this man this wisdom, and these mighty works? Is not this the carpenter's son? Is not his mother called Mary? And his brethren, James, and Joses, and Simon, and Judas? And his sisters, are they not all with us? Whence then hath this man all these things? And they were offended in him. But Jesus said unto them, a prophet is not without honour, save in his own country, and in his own house. And he did not many mighty works there because of their unbelief.

Matthew 13:53-58

2546. The force of *inner* prosperity produces *outer* prosperity. As we intentionally work to develop our inner life and outer responses, then, we will determine the release of the wealth from within us.

To whom God would make known what is the riches of the glory of this mystery among the Gentiles; which is Christ in you, the hope of glory.

Colossians 1:27

2547. Regarding advice for success, don't listen to *zeros*, when you know you're *100%*!

He that is despised, and hath a servant, is better than he that honoureth himself, and lacketh bread.

Proverbs 12:9

2548. Learn from proven leaders. Follow the faithful. Imitate the preeminent. Chase the champions. Be transformed by the trainers. Reach your destiny.

That ye be not slothful, but followers of them who through faith and patience inherit the promises.

Hebrews 6:12

2549. Practice peace. It's a key to mental, emotional, and physical health. Continue to cast your cares upon the Lord. Don't carry the heavy emotional load. You can be responsible, and yet be actively, intentionally casting the concern of your responsibility over on the Lord. Your level of intimacy will increase with the Lord, because you will grow to depend upon him. Practice peace. It's the key to long-term health.

Thou wilt keep him in perfect peace, whose mind is stayed on thee: because he trusteth in thee. Trust ye in the Lord for ever: for in the Lord Jehovah is everlasting strength.

Isaiah 26:3-4

2550. Regarding the pursuit of success, you're not in competition with anyone else. God gives each of us opportunity to succeed, according to our individual strengths, gifts, and talents. The only way that someone else could get your reward is if you failed to pursue what God gave you in *seed* form. If you fail to tend to your potential harvest, God may give it to someone else who will be a better steward, and will multiply it.

For the kingdom of heaven is as a man travelling into a far country, who called his own servants, and delivered unto them his goods. And unto one he gave five talents, to another two, and to another one; to every man according to his several ability; and straightway took his journey. Then he that had received the five talents went and traded with the same, and made them other five talents. And likewise he that had received two, he also gained other two. But he that had received one went and digged in the earth, and hid his Lord's money. After a long time the Lord of those servants cometh, and reckoneth with them. And so he that had received five talents came and brought other five talents, saying, Lord, thou deliveredst unto me five talents: behold, I have gained beside them five talents more. His Lord said unto him, well done, thou good and faithful servant: thou hast been faithful over a few things, I will make thee ruler over many things: enter

thou into the joy of thy Lord. He also that had received two talents came and said, Lord, thou deliveredst unto me two talents: behold, I have gained two other talents beside them. His Lord said unto him, well done, good and faithful servant; thou hast been faithful over a few things, I will make thee ruler over many things: enter thou into the joy of thy Lord. Then he which had received the one talent came and said, Lord, I knew thee that thou art an hard man, reaping where thou hast not sown, and gathering where thou hast not strawed: And I was afraid, and went and hid thy talent in the earth: lo, there thou hast that is thine. His Lord answered and said unto him, thou wicked and slothful servant, thou knewest that I reap where I sowed not, and gather where I have not strawed: Thou oughtest therefore to have put my money to the exchangers, and then at my coming I should have received mine own with usury. Take therefore the talent from him, and give it unto him, which hath ten talents. For unto every one that hath shall be given, and he shall have abundance: but from him that hath not shall be taken away even that which he hath.

Matthew 25:14-29

2551. Regarding the importance of money, succeeding is the best thing that you can do for everyone involved. Without money you can't help anybody for any sustained period of time in any practical way.

A feast is made for laughter, and wine maketh merry: but money answereth all things.

Ecclesiastes 10:19

2552. Being thankful feels better than complaining for everybody involved.

Rejoice evermore. Pray without ceasing. In every thing give thanks: for this is the will of God in Christ Jesus concerning you.

1 Thessalonians 5:16-18

2553. Being thankful preps you for the future. Complaining traps you in the past.

And David was greatly distressed; for the people spake of stoning him, because the soul of all the people was grieved, every man for his sons and for his daughters: but David encouraged himself in the Lord his God.

1 Samuel 30:6

2554. Never listen to small-minded critics about your dreams, because they will pressure you to shrink your dream to fit their expectations.

And Joseph dreamed a dream, and he told it his brethren: and they hated him yet the more. And he said unto them, hear, I pray you, this dream which I have dreamed: for, behold, we were binding sheaves in the field, and, lo, my sheaf arose, and also stood upright; and, behold, your sheaves stood round about, and made obeisance to my sheaf. And his brethren said

to him, shalt thou indeed reign over us? Or shalt thou indeed have dominion over us? And they hated him yet the more for his dreams, and for his words. And he dreamed yet another dream, and told it his brethren, and said, behold, I have dreamed a dream more; and, behold, the sun and the moon and the eleven stars made obeisance to me. And he told it to his father, and to his brethren: and his father rebuked him, and said unto him, what is this dream that thou hast dreamed? Shall I and thy mother and thy brethren indeed come to bow down ourselves to thee to the earth? And his brethren envied him; but his father observed the saying.

Genesis 37:5-11

2555. Life can be tough. It can be busy. However, you do get out of it what you put into it. You must have a sense of direction. You must have a sense of *mission* in order to make your life interesting. It's really bad if you feel that you have nowhere to be, nowhere to go, and nothing to do. Therefore, no matter how challenging your life may be, you should be thankful for the life that you have.

Rejoice evermore. Pray without ceasing. In every thing give thanks: for this is the will of God in Christ Jesus concerning you.

1 Thessalonians 5:16-18

2556. Learning time is not selling time.

And that ye study to be quiet, and to do your own business, and to work with your own hands, as we commanded you; that ye may walk honestly toward them that are without, and that ye may have lack of nothing.

1 Thessalonians 4:11-12

2557. Avoid unnecessary words today. Rather, let your work and results speak for you. Let discretion guide you. Let your excellence speak for you today.

For a dream cometh through the multitude of business; and a fool's voice is known by multitude of words.

Ecclesiastes 5:3

2558. Regarding your destiny, don't get disheartened. Don't get dismayed. Don't get discouraged. You have a great distance to explore and enjoy in your land of promise and you have many years of enjoyment in it.

If they obey and serve him, they shall spend their days in prosperity, and their years in pleasures.

Job 36:11

2559. Mothers are a gift that keeps on giving far after your required growing-up years. Therefore, be sure to give your mother, your wife, and other honorable women in your life, a gift that will keep on giving to them. Show them your love in a very tangible way for Mother's Day. They deserve it!

Who can find a virtuous woman? For her price is far above rubies. The heart of her husband doth safely trust in her, so that he shall have no need of spoil. She will do him good and not evil all the days of her life. She seeketh wool, and flax, and worketh willingly with her hands. She is like the merchants' ships; she bringeth her food from afar. She riseth also while it is yet night, and giveth meat to her household, and a portion to her maidens. She considereth a field, and buyeth it: with the fruit of her hands she planteth a vineyard. She girdeth her loins with strength, and strengtheneth her arms. She perceiveth that her merchandise is good: her candle goeth not out by night. She layeth her hands to the spindle, and her hands hold the distaff. She stretcheth out her hand to the poor; yea, she reacheth forth her hands to the needy. She is not afraid of the snow for her household: for all her household are clothed with scarlet. She maketh herself coverings of tapestry; her clothing is silk and purple. Her husband is known in the gates, when he sitteth among the elders of the land. She maketh fine linen, and selleth it; and delivereth girdles unto the merchant. Strength and honour are her clothing; and she shall rejoice in time to come. She openeth her mouth with wisdom; and in her tongue is the law of kindness. She looketh well to the ways of her household, and eateth not the bread of idleness. Her children arise up, and call her blessed; her husband also, and he praiseth her. Many daughters have done virtuously, but thou excellest them all. Favour is deceitful, and beauty is vain: but a woman that feareth the Lord, she shall be praised. Give her of the fruit of her hands; and let her own works praise her in the gates.

Proverbs 31:10-31

2560. Regarding complaints about your job, when you know that your money depends on it, then, you will change.

And whatsoever ye do, do it heartily, as to the Lord, and not unto men; knowing that of the Lord ye shall receive the reward of the inheritance: for ye serve the Lord Christ.

Colossians 3:23-24

2561. Do what's required to obtain what's desired today. Let your light so very much shine before the world. Represent your Heavenly Father well. Be an example of Jesus Christ in all that you do. Have a good day today.

Wherefore, my beloved, as ye have always obeyed, not as in my presence only, but now much more in my absence, work out your own salvation with fear and trembling. For it is God which worketh in you both to will and to do of his good pleasure. Do all things without murmurings and disputings: that ye may be blameless and harmless, the sons of God, without rebuke, in the midst of a crooked and perverse nation, among whom ye shine as lights in the world; holding forth the word of life; that I may rejoice in the day of Christ, that I have not run in vain, neither laboured in vain.

Philippians 2:12-16

2562. Keep on praying. Keep on giving. Keep on living right. Your lifestyle before God is drawing the presence of the Holy Spirit into the earth. Your devotion to God is making room for His Spirit to move in places He may not have at first

been welcomed. You are a conduit of God's grace and love. Keep praying. You're making a difference!

There was a certain man in Caesarea called Cornelius, a centurion of the band called the Italian band, A devout man, and one that feared God with all his house, which gave much alms to the people, and prayed to God alway. He saw in a vision evidently about the ninth hour of the day an angel of God coming in to him, and saying unto him, Cornelius. And when he looked on him, he was afraid, and said, what is it, Lord? And he said unto him, thy prayers and thine alms are come up for a memorial before God. And now send men to Joppa, and call for one Simon, whose surname is Peter: He lodgeth with one Simon a tanner, whose house is by the seaside: he shall tell thee what thou oughtest to do. And when the angel which spake unto Cornelius was departed, he called two of his household servants, and a devout soldier of them that waited on him continually; And when he had declared all these things unto them, he sent them to Joppa. On the morrow, as they went on their journey, and drew nigh unto the city, Peter went up upon the housetop to pray about the sixth hour: And he became very hungry, and would have eaten: but while they made ready, he fell into a trance, And saw heaven opened, and a certain vessel descending upon him, as it had been a great sheet knit at the four corners, and let down to the earth: Wherein were all manner of four-footed beasts of the earth, and wild beasts, and creeping things, and fowls of the air. And there came a voice to him, rise, Peter; kill, and eat. But Peter said, not so, Lord; for I have never eaten any thing that is common or unclean. And the voice spake unto him again the second time, what God hath

Pastor Terrance Levise Turner, MBA

cleansed, that call not thou common. This was done thrice: and the vessel was received up again into heaven. Now while Peter doubted in himself what this vision which he had seen should mean, behold, the men which were sent from Cornelius had made enquiry for Simon's house, and stood before the gate, And called, and asked whether Simon, which was surnamed Peter, were lodged there. While Peter thought on the vision, the spirit said unto him, behold, three men seek thee. Arise therefore, and get thee down, and go with them, doubting nothing: for I have sent them. Then Peter went down to the men, which were sent unto him from Cornelius; and said, behold, I am he whom ye seek: what is the cause wherefore ye are come? And they said, Cornelius the centurion, a just man, and one that feareth God, and of good report among all the nation of the Jews, was warned from God by an holy angel to send for thee into his house, and to hear words of thee. Then called he them in, and lodged them. And on the morrow Peter went away with them, and certain brethren from Joppa accompanied him. And the morrow after they entered into Caesarea. And Cornelius waited for them, and he had called together his kinsmen and near friends. And as Peter was coming in, Cornelius met him, and fell down at his feet, and worshipped him. But Peter took him up, saying, stand up; I myself also am a man. And as he talked with him, he went in, and found many that were come together. And he said unto them, ye know how that it is an unlawful thing for a man that is a Jew to keep company, or come unto one of another nation; but God hath shewed me that I should not call any man common or unclean. Therefore came I unto you without gainsaying, as soon as I was sent for: I ask therefore for what intent ye have sent for me? And Cornelius said, four

days ago I was fasting until this hour; and at the ninth hour I prayed in my house, and, behold, a man stood before me in bright clothing, And said, Cornelius, thy prayer is heard, and thine alms are had in remembrance in the sight of God. Send therefore to Joppa, and call hither Simon, whose surname is Peter; he is lodged in the house of one Simon a tanner by the seaside: who, when he cometh, shall speak unto thee. Immediately therefore I sent to thee; and thou hast well done that thou art come. Now therefore are we all here present before God, to hear all things that are commanded thee of God. Then Peter opened his mouth, and said, of a truth I perceive that God is no respecter of persons: But in every nation he that feareth him, and worketh righteousness, is accepted with him. The word which God sent unto the children of Israel, preaching peace by Jesus Christ: (he is Lord of all:) That word, I say, ye know, which was published throughout all Judaea, and began from galilee, after the baptism which John preached; How God anointed Jesus of Nazareth with the Holy Ghost and with power: who went about doing good, and healing all that were oppressed of the devil; for God was with him. And we are witnesses of all things which he did both in the land of the Jews, and in Jerusalem; whom they slew and hanged on a tree: Him God raised up the third day, and shewed him openly; Not to all the people, but unto witnesses chosen before God, even to us, who did eat and drink with him after he rose from the dead. And he commanded us to preach unto the people, and to testify that it is he, which was ordained of God to be the judge of quick and dead. To him give all the prophets witness, that through his name whosoever believeth in him shall receive remission of sins. While Peter yet spake these words, the

Holy Ghost fell on all them, which heard the word. And they of the circumcision, which believed, were astonished, as many as came with Peter, because that on the gentiles also was poured out the gift of the Holy Ghost. For they heard them speak with tongues, and magnify God. Then answered Peter, Can any man forbid water, that these should not be baptized, which have received the Holy Ghost as well as we? And he commanded them to be baptized in the name of the Lord. Then prayed they him to tarry certain days.

Acts 10

2563. In a world of accelerating change the key to winning the game of life is to always be on the *offense*. Organizations are looking for employees who *embrace* change. To stay relevant you must be a part of the *genesis of change*!

But thou, O Daniel, shut up the words, and seal the book, even to the time of the end: many shall run to and fro, and knowledge shall be increased.

Daniel 12:4

2564. Keep on praying. If things are looking good, then, keep on praying. If things are looking bad, then, keep on praying. Never get so relaxed, disappointed, or dismayed that you stop praying. Prayer changes things in your favor. Prayer maintains the victory. Keep on praying!

And he spake a parable unto them *to this end*, that men ought always to pray, and not to faint.

Distinguished Wisdom Presents . . . "Living Proverbs"–Vol.5

Luke 18:1

2565. Here are keys to successful visualization: 1) See the outcome that you desire. 2) See the objections and obstacles. 3) Overcome the objections and obstacles successfully in your mind. 4) See your finished goal accomplished.

And it came to pass, when Rachel had born Joseph, that Jacob said unto Laban, send me away, that I may go unto mine own place, and to my country. Give me my wives and my children, for whom I have served thee, and let me go: for thou knowest my service, which I have done thee. And Laban said unto him, I pray thee, if I have found favour in thine eyes, tarry: for I have learned by experience that the Lord hath blessed me for thy sake. And he said, appoint me thy wages, and I will give it. And he said unto him, thou knowest how I have served thee, and how thy cattle was with me. For it was little which thou hadst before I came, and it is now increased unto a multitude; and the Lord hath blessed thee since my coming: and now when shall I provide for mine own house also? And he said, what shall I give thee? And Jacob said, thou shalt not give me any thing: if thou wilt do this thing for me, I will again feed and keep thy flock. I will pass through all thy flock to day, removing from thence all the speckled and spotted cattle, and all the brown cattle among the sheep, and the spotted and speckled among the goats: and of such shall be my hire. So shall my righteousness answer for me in time to come, when it shall come for my hire before thy face: every one that is not speckled and spotted among the goats, and brown among the sheep, that shall be counted stolen with me. And Laban said, behold, I would it might be according to thy word. And he

removed that day the he goats that were ringstraked and spotted, and all the she goats that were speckled and spotted, and every one that had some white in it, and all the brown among the sheep, and gave them into the hand of his sons. And he set three days' journey betwixt himself and Jacob: and Jacob fed the rest of Laban's flocks. And Jacob took him rods of green poplar, and of the hazel and chestnut tree; and pilled white strakes in them, and made the white appear which was in the rods. And he set the rods, which he had pilled before the flocks in the gutters in the watering troughs when the flocks came to drink, that they should conceive when they came to drink. And the flocks conceived before the rods, and brought forth cattle ringstraked, speckled, and spotted. And Jacob did separate the lambs, and set the faces of the flocks toward the ringstraked, and all the brown in the flock of Laban; and he put his own flocks by themselves, and put them not unto Laban's cattle. And it came to pass, whensoever the stronger cattle did conceive, that Jacob laid the rods before the eyes of the cattle in the gutters, that they might conceive among the rods. But when the cattle were feeble, he put them not in: so the feebler were Laban's, and the stronger Jacob's. And the man increased exceedingly, and had much cattle, and maidservants, and menservants, and camels, and asses.

Genesis 30:25-43

2566. Thank God for strong women who know how to obey God. A strong woman of God can save nations!

And the king of Egypt spake to the Hebrew midwives, of which the name of the one was Shiphrah, and the name of the

other Puah: And he said, when ye do the office of a midwife to the Hebrew women, and see them upon the stools; if it be a son, then ye shall kill him: but if it be a daughter, then she shall live. But the midwives feared God, and did not as the king of Egypt commanded them, but saved the men children alive. And the king of Egypt called for the midwives, and said unto them, why have ye done this thing, and have saved the men children alive? And the midwives said unto pharaoh, because the Hebrew women are not as the Egyptian women; for they are lively, and are delivered ere the midwives come in unto them. Therefore God dealt well with the midwives: and the people multiplied, and waxed very mighty. And it came to pass, because the midwives feared God, that he made them houses.

Exodus 1:15-21

2567. In many cases, singers and songwriters are the prophets and sages of the ages.

Now these be the last words of David. David the son of Jesse said, and the man who was raised up on high, the anointed of the God of Jacob, and the sweet Psalmist of Israel, said, the spirit of the Lord spake by me, and his word was in my tongue.

2 Samuel 23:1-2

2568. Regarding pricing, if the potential customer doesn't perceive your product valuable enough to pay your set price, then, don't change your price, rather, change the customers

that you pursue. Find a customer that recognizes, perceives, and desires the value that your product or service provides, so much so, that they will be glad and willing to pay your set price in order to obtain it.

My son, if thou wilt receive my words, and hide my commandments with thee; So that thou incline thine ear unto wisdom, and apply thine heart to understanding; Yea, if thou criest after knowledge, and liftest up thy voice for understanding; If thou seekest her as silver, and searchest for her as for hid treasures; Then shalt thou understand the fear of the Lord, and find the knowledge of God. For the Lord giveth wisdom: out of his mouth cometh knowledge and understanding. He layeth up sound wisdom for the righteous: he is a buckler to them that walk uprightly. He keepeth the paths of judgment, and preserveth the way of his saints. Then shalt thou understand righteousness, and judgment, and equity; yea, every good path. When wisdom entereth into thine heart, and knowledge is pleasant unto thy soul; discretion shall preserve thee, understanding shall keep thee.

Proverbs 2:1-11

2569. Just a word of encouragement: You are a champion! You have already won more battles than the average person. You have the crowns of victory. Be strong! Be bold! Be confident! Be calm. Be peaceful. Be cool. Be collected. God is in you. God is with you. God is for you! You're doing great! You've already overcome in life!

Ye are of God, little children, and have overcome them: because greater is he that is in you, than he that is in the world.

1 John 4:4

2570. When you're on the verge of the next level of success, things may become rough around the edges. You have to really push to get over the top success!

For a great door and effectual is opened unto me, and there are many adversaries.

1 Corinthians 16:9

2571. A regular habit of prayer and Bible study will help you keep all of the *marbles in the pouch*, and keep all of the *strands tightly tucked in*, and from blowing in the wind. Read the Bible and pray. It will help to bring stability to your day.

I beseech you therefore, brethren, by the mercies of God, that ye present your bodies a living sacrifice, holy, acceptable unto God, which is your reasonable service. And be not conformed to this world: but be ye transformed by the renewing of your mind, that ye may prove what is that good, and acceptable, and perfect, will of God.

Romans 12:1-2

2572. Always assume the best, until proven otherwise, and even if it is otherwise, God can make it otherwise.

And we know that all things work together for good to them that love God, to them who are the called according to his purpose.

Romans 8:28

2573. After listening to all of the rules, regulations, and formulas of success from all of the wise priests, prophets, and teachers, ultimately, the key to success in life is diligent obedience to God's success principles found in His Word, the Bible.

Let us hear the conclusion of the whole matter: fear God, and keep his commandments: for this is the whole duty of man. For God shall bring every work into judgment, with every secret thing, whether it be good, or whether it be evil.

Ecclesiastes 12:13-14

2574. Those who have achieved great success have always been willing to step pass the boundaries of what the mediocre have deemed permissible.

The crown of the wise is their riches: but the foolishness of fools is folly.

Proverbs 14:24

2575. The proof of wisdom is *results*.

The crown of the wise is their riches: but the foolishness of fools is folly.

Proverbs 14:24

2576. Be thankful for one thing at a time and for one day at a time, and you will never run out of reasons to be thankful.

Rejoice evermore. Pray without ceasing. In every thing give thanks: for this is the will of God in Christ Jesus concerning you.

1 Thessalonians 5:16-18

2577. Some people have the brains, but not the heart. They are very intelligent, and often technically skilled. However, they often haven't developed the heart of consideration for other people, so as to treat others with mutual respect. Their brains are trained to solve technical problems. Yet, their heart hasn't been developed to discern mutual respect for others, whom they often undervalue due to another's lack of a skill or knowledge, which they possess. However, their lack of discernment demonstrates a lack of maturity in an essential skill: People skills. There are some things that a soul must discern beyond *brain* training. It must be developed in the heart.

Who is a wise man and endued with knowledge among you? Let him shew out of a good conversation his works with meekness of wisdom. But if ye have bitter envying and strife in your hearts, glory not, and lie not against the truth. This

wisdom descendeth not from above, but is earthly, sensual, devilish. For where envying and strife is, there is confusion and every evil work. But the wisdom that is from above is first pure, then peaceable, gentle, and easy to be intreated, full of mercy and good fruits, without partiality, and without hypocrisy. And the fruit of righteousness is sown in peace of them that make peace.

James 3:13-18

2578. It takes preparation and *execution* to attain profitability.

And that ye study to be quiet, and to do your own business, and to work with your own hands, as we commanded you; that ye may walk honestly toward them that are without, and that ye may have lack of nothing.

1 Thessalonians 4:11-12

2579. If you keep on taking steps in the right direction, then, you'll reach your destiny. The destination is sure. You just must keep taking the specific steps that are necessary, and you will certainly reach your destiny.

The steps of a good man are ordered by the Lord: and he delighteth in his way.

Psalm 37:23

2580. Regarding love, love is clear. You can see it if it exists, and you can clearly see if it doesn't. God is love.

Charity suffereth long, and is kind; charity envieth not; charity vaunteth not itself, is not puffed up, Doth not behave itself unseemly, seeketh not her own, is not easily provoked, thinketh no evil; Rejoiceth not in iniquity, but rejoiceth in the truth; Beareth all things, believeth all things, hopeth all things, endureth all things. Charity never faileth: but whether there be prophecies, they shall fail; whether there be tongues, they shall cease; whether there be knowledge, it shall vanish away. For we know in part, and we prophesy in part. But when that which is perfect is come, then that which is in part shall be done away. When I was a child, I spake as a child, I understood as a child, I thought as a child: but when I became a man, I put away childish things. For now we see through a glass, darkly; but then face to face: now I know in part; but then shall I know even as also I am known. And now abideth faith, hope, charity, these three; but the greatest of these is charity.

1 Corinthians 13:4-13

2581. Regarding prayer, prayer changes things, and God's grace changes people. You obtain grace through prayer.

For the word of God is quick, and powerful, and sharper than any twoedged sword, piercing even to the dividing asunder of soul and spirit, and of the joints and marrow, and is a discerner of the thoughts and intents of the heart. Neither is there any creature that is not manifest in his sight: but all

things are naked and opened unto the eyes of him with whom we have to do. Seeing then that we have a great high priest, that is passed into the heavens, Jesus the son of God, let us hold fast our profession. For we have not an high priest which cannot be touched with the feeling of our infirmities; but was in all points tempted like as we are, yet without sin. Let us therefore come boldly unto the throne of grace, that we may obtain mercy, and find grace to help in time of need.

Hebrews 4:12-16

2582. Regarding luxury houses and cars, the people that you have to share it with is more important than the house or the car. You could be living in a luxury home or driving a luxury car, but you could be living in it *alone*. You could be driving alone. But, if you have someone to share that love with, then, it's more important than anything else. It's more about the people that you have to share it with, than it is the luxury home or car. Learn to enjoy the people that you love.

Better is little with the fear of the Lord than great treasure and trouble therewith. Better is a dinner of herbs where love is, than a stalled ox and hatred therewith.

Proverbs 15:16-17

2583. Keep your passion alive, because that's the *fuel* that you need for the drive to arrive at your destination.

So then faith cometh by hearing, and hearing by the word of God.

Romans 10:17

2584. Regarding criticism, you have to evaluate criticism based on the level from which it's coming. If it's coming from a lower level than who you are, then you don't have to pay too much attention to it, because it hasn't risen to the level of importance or significance that merits very much response. If you know you're operating from a higher level of responsibility, just respond according to who you are and what you know you do, rather than low-level criticism.

He that is despised, and hath a servant, is better than he that honoureth himself, and lacketh bread.

Proverbs 12:9

2585. Don't focus on your problems. Focus on your blessings. If you focus on your blessings, your blessings will multiply.

The blessing of the Lord, it maketh rich, and he addeth no sorrow with it.

Proverbs 10:22

2586. Sleep helps you get all the *marbles* back in the pouch!

It is vain for you to rise up early, to sit up late, to eat the bread of sorrows: for so he giveth his beloved sleep.

Psalms 126:2

Pastor Terrance Levise Turner, MBA

2587. Don't be afraid to try new things. You only have one life to live. Make it as interesting as you can.

For to him that is joined to all the living there is hope: for a living dog is better than a dead lion. For the living know that they shall die: but the dead know not any thing, neither have they any more a reward; for the memory of them is forgotten. Also their love, and their hatred, and their envy, is now perished; neither have they any more a portion for ever in any thing that is done under the sun. Go thy way, eat thy bread with joy, and drink thy wine with a merry heart; for God now accepteth thy works. Let thy garments be always white; and let thy head lack no ointment. Live joyfully with the wife whom thou lovest all the days of the life of thy vanity, which he hath given thee under the sun, all the days of thy vanity: for that is thy portion in this life, and in thy labour which thou takest under the sun. Whatsoever thy hand findeth to do, do it with thy might; for there is no work, nor device, nor knowledge, nor wisdom, in the grave, whither thou goest. I returned, and saw under the sun, that the race is not to the swift, nor the battle to the strong, neither yet bread to the wise, nor yet riches to men of understanding, nor yet favour to men of skill; but time and chance happeneth to them all.

Ecclesiastes 9:4-11

2588. If you want to change, then, you have to change your mind.

I beseech you therefore, brethren, by the mercies of God, that ye present your bodies a living sacrifice, holy, acceptable unto

God, which is your reasonable service. And be not conformed to this world: but be ye transformed by the renewing of your mind, that ye may prove what is that good, and acceptable, and perfect, will of God.

Romans 12:1-2

2589. No matter how complex your life or thinking becomes, you're never beyond being able to worship God. God made you. It is clear that you didn't make yourself. It is obvious that you don't have power to keep yourself alive. God opened your eyes this morning. He kept your heart beating during the night. Give Him the praise for Who He is. He is Almighty God!

Praise ye the Lord. Praise ye the Lord from the heavens: praise him in the heights. Praise ye him, all his angels: praise ye him, all his hosts. Praise ye him, sun and moon: praise him, all ye stars of light. Praise him, ye heavens of heavens, and ye waters that be above the heavens. Let them praise the name of the Lord: for he commanded, and they were created. He hath also stablished them for ever and ever: he hath made a decree, which shall not pass. Praise the Lord from the earth, ye dragons, and all deeps: Fire, and hail; snow, and vapours; stormy wind fulfilling his word: Mountains, and all hills; fruitful trees, and all cedars: Beasts, and all cattle; creeping things, and flying fowl: Kings of the earth, and all people; princes, and all judges of the earth: Both young men, and maidens; old men, and children: Let them praise the name of the Lord: for his name alone is excellent; his glory is above the earth and heaven. He also exalteth the horn of his people, the

praise of all his saints; even of the children of Israel, a people near unto him. Praise ye the Lord.

Psalm 148

2590. Uniqueness increases value. Rarity is an advantage. Be yourself. You are the *star* in your own sky. Let your light shine upon the world. Help to give life to the world surrounding you!

Ye are the salt of the earth: but if the salt have lost his savour, wherewith shall it be salted? It is thenceforth good for nothing, but to be cast out, and to be trodden under foot of men. Ye are the light of the world. A city that is set on an hill cannot be hid. Neither do men light a candle, and put it under a bushel, but on a candlestick; and it giveth light unto all that are in the house. Let your light so shine before men, that they may see your good works, and glorify your father, which is in heaven.

Matthew 5:13-16

2591. Being thankful solves so many ails of life.

Rejoice in the Lord always: and again I say, rejoice. Let your moderation be known unto all men. The Lord is at hand. Be careful for nothing; but in every thing by prayer and supplication with thanksgiving let your requests be made known unto God. And the peace of God, which passeth all understanding, shall keep your hearts and minds through Christ Jesus. Finally, brethren, whatsoever things are true,

whatsoever things are honest, whatsoever things are just, whatsoever things are pure, whatsoever things are lovely, whatsoever things are of good report; if there be any virtue, and if there be any praise, think on these things. Those things, which ye have both learned, and received, and heard, and seen in me, do: and the God of peace shall be with you.

Philippians 4:4-9

2592. When your life starts to get out of control, then, that's a sign that you have neglected the spiritual disciplines of worship, prayer, Bible meditation, biblical confessions, and fasting. We are a spirit. We live in a body. We have a soul. All of life balance comes from spiritual balance.

Therefore whosoever heareth these sayings of mine, and doeth them, I will liken him unto a wise man, which built his house upon a rock: And the rain descended, and the floods came, and the winds blew, and beat upon that house; and it fell not: for it was founded upon a rock. And every one that heareth these sayings of mine, and doeth them not, shall be likened unto a foolish man, which built his house upon the sand: And the rain descended, and the floods came, and the winds blew, and beat upon that house; and it fell: and great was the fall of it.

Matthew 7:24-27

2593. Regarding the state of the economy, stop complaining and *get busy*! The surplus profit of the earth is for all. The king

himself is served by the surplus profit, derived from a cultivated, educated, and skillful populace.

Moreover, the profit of the earth is for all; the king himself is served by the field *and* in all, a king is an advantage to a land with cultivated fields.

Ecclesiastes 5:9

Amplified Bible, Classic Edition (AMPC)

2594. Be very watchful and circumspect regarding the companionships that you take on and the places you go with them. Everyone's plans and intentions may not be as pure as they seem. Most things are never as harmless as they appear. Always learn from the past experiences of others, so that your life doesn't become a tale of caution to those coming after you.

The simple believeth every word: but the prudent man looketh well to his going.

Proverbs 14:15

2595. Treat everybody well, from the highest to the lowest, from the richest to the poorest. Treat everybody well.

The rich and poor meet together: the Lord is the maker of them all.

Proverbs 22:2

2596. The only thing that stands in between you and millions, or even billions of dollars, is your execution of your God-given ideas. Expertise can be purchased or hired, but ideas must be inspired and acted upon!

Now faith is the substance of things hoped for, the evidence of things not seen. For by it the elders obtained a good report.

Hebrews 11:1-2

2597. Regarding winning and becoming a winner, no pouting, no doubting, and no quitting are the keys. In the face of disappointment, you may pout temporarily, but snap out of it! In the face of seemingly insurmountable odds, you may doubt periodically, but build your faith to overcome it. In the face of a dream that seems beyond your current grasp, don't quit! These are the keys to winning and becoming a winner!

I can do all things through Christ, which strengtheneth me.

Philippians 4:13

2598. God is good. God loves you. God wants you to prosper.

Beloved, I wish above all things that thou mayest prosper and be in health, even as thy soul prospereth.

3 John 2

2599. Throw out the pendulum of obedience. Then, believe God for the return of the harvest of His goodness into your life.

The desire of the righteous is only good: but the expectation of the wicked is wrath. There is that scattereth, and yet increaseth; and there is that withholdeth more than is meet, but it tendeth to poverty. The liberal soul shall be made fat: and he that watereth shall be watered also himself. He that withholdeth corn, the people shall curse him: but blessing shall be upon the head of him that selleth it. He that diligently seeketh good procureth favour: but he that seeketh mischief, it shall come unto him.

Proverbs 11:23-27

2600. Religion is a tool that is used to comfort, control, and pacify people in their complacency and inactivity as they circle around in a pasture of inadequacy for years and years. However, *wisdom* is the principal thing needed to get out of the *rut* and move forward with your life. Wisdom, knowledge, and revelation will equip and motivate you to possess the land, rather than to only continue to talk about it and aspire to it. Believe in the Lord your God, so shall you be established. However, it takes *prophets of prosperity* to teach you and to lead you to *profit*. That's if you truly want to do what's required to obtain it.

And they rose early in the morning, and went forth into the wilderness of Tekoa: and as they went forth, Jehoshaphat stood and said, hear me, O Judah, and ye inhabitants of

Jerusalem; believe in the Lord your God, so shall ye be established; believe his prophets, so shall ye prosper.

2 Chronicles 20:20

2601. Refine your gifts and talents, and turn them into skills. Get your education. Put forth effort. And, you will guarantee a profitable result.

In all labour there is profit: but the talk of the lips tendeth only to penury.

Proverbs 14:23

2602. Criticism is a compliment from those who noticed you, but were too negative to compliment you.

It is naught, it is naught, saith the buyer: but when he is gone his way, then he boasteth.

Proverbs 20:14

2603. May God strengthen you to be a true *contender* in life. May you be able to withstand the bouts for the *heavyweight championships of the world*. Someone has to be champion in life. May one of them be you!

Beloved, when I gave all diligence to write unto you of the common salvation, it was needful for me to write unto you, and exhort you that ye should earnestly contend for the faith, which was once delivered unto the saints.

Jude 1:3

2604. Practice loving yourself. Others will love you like *you* love you.

I will praise thee; for I am fearfully and wonderfully made: marvellous are thy works; and that my soul knoweth right well.

Psalm 139:14

2605. Your investments into improvement demonstrate your level of commitment.

Buy the truth, and sell it not; also wisdom, and instruction, and understanding.

Proverbs 23:23

2606. Regarding the critics of your *success schedule*, people who haven't sown any seed toward your success have no right to evaluate your success schedule. Your ultimate success is between your own efforts and God's divine favor.

But let every man prove his own work, and then shall he have rejoicing in himself alone, and not in another.

Galatians 6:4

2607. A wise wife realizes that her inheritance is in her husband's heritage. That's why she took his last name.

Distinguished Wisdom Presents . . . "Living Proverbs"–Vol.5

And Abraham was old, and well stricken in age: and the Lord had blessed Abraham in all things. And Abraham said unto his eldest servant of his house, that ruled over all that he had, put, I pray thee, thy hand under my thigh: And I will make thee swear by the Lord, the God of heaven, and the God of the earth, that thou shalt not take a wife unto my son of the daughters of the Canaanites, among whom I dwell: But thou shalt go unto my country, and to my kindred, and take a wife unto my son Isaac. And the servant said unto him, peradventure the woman will not be willing to follow me unto this land: must I needs bring thy son again unto the land from whence thou camest? And Abraham said unto him, beware thou that thou bring not my son thither again. The Lord God of heaven, which took me from my father's house, and from the land of my kindred, and which spake unto me, and that sware unto me, saying, unto thy seed will I give this land; he shall send his angel before thee, and thou shalt take a wife unto my son from thence. And if the woman will not be willing to follow thee, then thou shalt be clear from this my oath: only bring not my son thither again. And the servant put his hand under the thigh of Abraham his master, and sware to him concerning that matter. And the servant took ten camels of the camels of his master, and departed; for all the goods of his master were in his hand: and he arose, and went to Mesopotamia, unto the city of Nahor. And he made his camels to kneel down without the city by a well of water at the time of the evening, even the time that women go out to draw water. And he said o Lord God of my master Abraham, I pray thee, send me good speed this day, and shew kindness unto my master Abraham. Behold, I stand here by the well of water; and the daughters of the men of the city come out to

draw water: And let it come to pass, that the damsel to whom I shall say, let down thy pitcher, I pray thee, that I may drink; and she shall say, drink, and I will give thy camels drink also: let the same be she that thou hast appointed for thy servant Isaac; and thereby shall I know that thou hast shewed kindness unto my master. And it came to pass, before he had done speaking, that, behold, Rebekah came out, who was born to Bethuel, son of Milcah, the wife of Nahor, Abraham's brother, with her pitcher upon her shoulder. And the damsel was very fair to look upon, a virgin, neither had any man known her: and she went down to the well, and filled her pitcher, and came up. And the servant ran to meet her, and said, let me, I pray thee, drink a little water of thy pitcher. And she said, drink, my Lord: and she hasted, and let down her pitcher upon her hand, and gave him drink. And when she had done giving him drink, she said, I will draw water for thy camels also, until they have done drinking. And she hasted, and emptied her pitcher into the trough, and ran again unto the well to draw water, and drew for all his camels. And the man wondering at her held his peace, to wit whether the Lord had made his journey prosperous or not. And it came to pass, as the camels had done drinking, that the man took a golden earring of half a shekel weight, and two bracelets for her hands of ten shekels weight of gold; And said, whose daughter art thou? Tell me, I pray thee: is there room in thy father's house for us to lodge in? And she said unto him, I am the daughter of Bethuel the son of Milcah, which she bare unto Nahor. She said moreover unto him, we have both straw and provender enough, and room to lodge in. And the man bowed down his head, and worshipped the Lord. And he said, blessed be the Lord God of my master Abraham, who hath not

left destitute my master of his mercy and his truth: I being in the way, the Lord led me to the house of my master's brethren. And the damsel ran, and told them of her mother's house these things. And Rebekah had a brother, and his name was Laban: and Laban ran out unto the man, unto the well. And it came to pass, when he saw the earring and bracelets upon his sister's hands, and when he heard the words of Rebekah his sister, saying, thus spake the man unto me; that he came unto the man; and, behold, he stood by the camels at the well. And he said, come in, thou blessed of the Lord; wherefore standest thou without? For I have prepared the house, and room for the camels. And the man came into the house: and he ungirded his camels, and gave straw and provender for the camels, and water to wash his feet, and the men's feet that were with him. And there was set meat before him to eat: but he said, I will not eat, until I have told mine errand. And he said, speak on. And he said, I am Abraham's servant. And the Lord hath blessed my master greatly; and he is become great: and he hath given him flocks, and herds, and silver, and gold, and menservants, and maidservants, and camels, and asses. And Sarah my master's wife bare a son to my master when she was old: and unto him hath he given all that he hath. And my master made me swear, saying, thou shalt not take a wife to my son of the daughters of the Canaanites, in whose land I dwell: But thou shalt go unto my father's house, and to my kindred, and take a wife unto my son. And I said unto my master, peradventure the woman will not follow me. And he said unto me, the Lord, before whom I walk, will send his angel with thee, and prosper thy way; and thou shalt take a wife for my son of my kindred, and of my father's house: Then shalt thou be clear from this my oath,

when thou comest to my kindred; and if they give not thee one, thou shalt be clear from my oath. And I came this day unto the well, and said, o Lord God of my master Abraham, if now thou do prosper my way, which I go: Behold, I stand by the well of water; and it shall come to pass, that when the virgin cometh forth to draw water, and I say to her, give me, I pray thee, a little water of thy pitcher to drink; And she say to me, both drink thou, and I will also draw for thy camels: let the same be the woman whom the Lord hath appointed out for my master's son. And before I had done speaking in mine heart, behold, Rebekah came forth with her pitcher on her shoulder; and she went down unto the well, and drew water: and I said unto her, let me drink, I pray thee. And she made haste, and let down her pitcher from her shoulder, and said, drink, and I will give thy camels drink also: so I drank, and she made the camels drink also. And I asked her, and said, whose daughter art thou? And she said, the daughter of Bethuel, Nahor's son, whom Milcah bare unto him: and I put the earring upon her face, and the bracelets upon her hands. And I bowed down my head, and worshipped the Lord, and blessed the Lord God of my master Abraham, which had led me in the right way to take my master's brother's daughter unto his son. And now if ye will deal kindly and truly with my master, tell me: and if not, tell me; that I may turn to the right hand, or to the left. Then Laban and Bethuel answered and said, the thing proceedeth from the Lord: we cannot speak unto thee bad or good. Behold, Rebekah is before thee, take her, and go, and let her be thy master's son's wife, as the Lord hath spoken. And it came to pass, that, when Abraham's servant heard their words, he worshipped the Lord, bowing himself to the earth. And the servant brought forth jewels of

silver, and jewels of gold, and raiment, and gave them to Rebekah: he gave also to her brother and to her mother precious things. And they did eat and drink, he and the men that were with him, and tarried all night; and they rose up in the morning, and he said, send me away unto my master. And her brother and her mother said, let the damsel abide with us a few days, at the least ten; after that she shall go. And he said unto them, hinder me not, seeing the Lord hath prospered my way; send me away that I may go to my master. And they said, we will call the damsel, and enquire at her mouth. And they called Rebekah, and said unto her, wilt thou go with this man? And she said, I will go. And they sent away Rebekah their sister, and her nurse, and Abraham's servant, and his men. And they blessed Rebekah, and said unto her, thou art our sister, be thou the mother of thousands of millions, and let thy seed possess the gate of those which hate them. And Rebekah arose, and her damsels, and they rode upon the camels, and followed the man: and the servant took Rebekah, and went his way. And Isaac came from the way of the well Lahairoi; for he dwelt in the south country. And Isaac went out to meditate in the field at the eventide: and he lifted up his eyes, and saw, and, behold, the camels were coming. And Rebekah lifted up her eyes, and when she saw Isaac, she lighted off the camel. For she had said unto the servant, what man is this that walketh in the field to meet us? And the servant had said, it is my master: therefore she took a vail, and covered herself. And the servant told Isaac all things that he had done. And Isaac brought her into his mother Sarah's tent, and took Rebekah, and she became his wife; and he loved her: and Isaac was comforted after his mother's death.

Genesis 24

2608. Expectation will determine destination. Get in a place where your expectation is shaped for a better future. Stretch your expectation. Shape your expectation for better, brighter, and more glorious days! If you do so, then your destination will change. Your destination will be better than you thought before. Your destination will be more beautiful and more fulfilling! Expectation will determine destination.

And the Lord answered me, and said, write the vision, and make it plain upon tables, that he may run that readeth it. For the vision is yet for an appointed time, but at the end it shall speak, and not lie: though it tarry, wait for it; because it will surely come, it will not tarry. Behold, his soul which is lifted up is not upright in him: but the just shall live by his faith.

Habakkuk 2:2-4

2609. Do not fear today. Put your trust in the Lord, and call on Him as your Savior. He will protect you and your family from the dangers in the world. He is your Rock and protection. Trust in Him today!

Thou shalt not be afraid for the terror by night; Nor for the arrow that flieth by day; nor for the pestilence that walketh in darkness; Nor for the destruction that wasteth at noonday. A thousand shall fall at thy side, and ten thousand at thy right hand; but it shall not come nigh thee. Only with thine eyes shalt thou behold and see the reward of the wicked. Because thou hast made the Lord, which is my refuge, even the most

high, thy habitation; there shall no evil befall thee, neither shall any plague come nigh thy dwelling. For he shall give his angels charge over thee, to keep thee in all thy ways. They shall bear thee up in their hands, lest thou dash thy foot against a stone.

Psalm 91:5-12

2610. Regarding your adversaries, often their contention against you is a matter of envy, because they know who you already are, and they fear who you may become.

And the patriarchs, moved with envy, sold Joseph into Egypt: but God was with him, And delivered him out of all his afflictions, and gave him favour and wisdom in the sight of Pharaoh king of Egypt; and he made him governor over Egypt and all his house.

Acts 7:9-10

2611. Regarding dealing with carnal-minded people, sometimes it's like walking through a *pit of cobras*. You have to be like a *flute-player*. Walk lightly and sensitively to their nature, so as to keep from being bitten. Wisdom is the key to safely making it to the other side.

Behold, I send you forth as sheep in the midst of wolves: be ye therefore wise as serpents, and harmless as doves.

Matthew 10:16

2612. Regarding the purchase of services, you can't buy *class*. It must come *free* with the purchase. Yet, you can always tell when it's *missing*.

These were more noble than those in Thessalonica, in that they received the word with all readiness of mind, and searched the scriptures daily, whether those things were so. Therefore many of them believed; also of honourable women which were Greeks, and of men, not a few.

Acts 17:11-12

2613. Brilliant minds reveal thoughts that benefit the masses. Love God and worship Him daily. He will give you access to His mind. His understanding is infinite. Share His thoughts with the world.

But the natural man receiveth not the things of the spirit of God: for they are foolishness unto him: neither can he know them, because they are spiritually discerned. But he that is spiritual judgeth all things, yet he himself is judged of no man. For who hath known the mind of the Lord, that he may instruct him? But we have the mind of Christ.

1 Corinthians 2:14-16

2614. A great man or a great woman shows his or her greatness by how he or she treats all people. For he or she recognizes the greatness in all people. We were all made in the image and likeness of God. We are all God's offspring. We are all the *gods* of the earth.

I have said, ye are gods; and all of you are children of the most high.

Psalm 82:6

2615. Regarding preaching, the best word is the Word that you obey.

If they obey and serve him, they shall spend their days in prosperity, and their years in pleasures.

Job 36:11

2616. Regarding making an impression, *results* always makes an impression.

Seest thou a man diligent in his business? He shall stand before kings; he shall not stand before mean men.

Proverbs 22:29

2617. Regarding business, anytime that your profits from your sales of goods and services to your end customer are required to go through the hands of middle-men before it eventually hits your hand, there's potential and high probability of stealing. The best way to guarantee maximum profit is direct sales and direct compensation.

A false balance is abomination to the Lord: but a just weight is his delight.

Proverbs 11:1

2618. Regarding business, certain inequities in business will cause an *artist* to change his or her name as a *sign* of their dissatisfaction with those inequities. Eventual change only comes through protestations against inequities.

A false balance is abomination to the Lord: but a just weight is his delight.

Proverbs 11:1

2619. Success takes *sustained* effort over time. The Bible says, "Be . . . followers of them who through faith and patience inherit the promises." In other words, success doesn't come without a fight, and success doesn't come overnight. Success takes sustained effort over time.

For God is not unrighteous to forget your work and labour of love, which ye have shewed toward his name, in that ye have ministered to the saints, and do minister. And we desire that every one of you do shew the same diligence to the full assurance of hope unto the end: That ye be not slothful, but followers of them who through faith and patience inherit the promises.

Hebrews 6:10-12

2620. Leadership is for service. Ruler-ship, power, authority, control, and advantage are only for a time and for a purpose. The purpose is for service to others. Those who have power, and properly use it, will be rewarded. Those who

abuse it will be appropriately judged. Leadership is for service.

And the Lord said, who then is that faithful and wise steward, whom his Lord shall make ruler over his household, to give them their portion of meat in due season? Blessed is that servant, whom his Lord when he cometh shall find so doing. Of a truth I say unto you, that he will make him ruler over all that he hath. But and if that servant say in his heart, my Lord delayeth his coming; and shall begin to beat the menservants and maidens, and to eat and drink, and to be drunken; The Lord of that servant will come in a day when he looketh not for him, and at an hour when he is not aware, and will cut him in sunder, and will appoint him his portion with the unbelievers. And that servant, which knew his Lord's will, and prepared not himself, neither did according to his will, shall be beaten with many stripes. But he that knew not, and did commit things worthy of stripes, shall be beaten with few stripes. For unto whomsoever much is given, of him shall be much required: and to whom men have committed much, of him they will ask the more.

Luke 12:42-48

2621. One of the secrets of prayer is that it may be painful to pray and hold on through the midnight hour. However, if you hold on, then, you can be sure that your answer will show up in the morning light. God will either give you the wisdom to solve your problem or give you the strength to bear your way through it. Either way, joy will come in the morning light!

For his anger endureth but a moment; in his favour is life: weeping may endure for a night, but joy cometh in the morning.

Psalm 30:5

2622. Regarding mistakes, not every infraction require correction. Sometimes infractions require *compassion* to make things better.

The Lord hath appeared of old unto me, saying, yea, I have loved thee with an everlasting love: therefore with lovingkindness have I drawn thee.

Jeremiah 31:3

2623. Regarding problems, don't just say, "It's going to be alright." It's not going to be alright unless you *do what's right*. Problems require action to solve them.

To do justice and judgment is more acceptable to the Lord than sacrifice.

Proverbs 21:3

2624. Be encouraged. God has it under control, even when it's out of *our* control.

Behold, the Lord's hand is not shortened, that it cannot save; neither his ear heavy, that it cannot hear.

Isaiah 59:1

2625. Solve problems quickly before you're *forced* to solve them, because when the problems arise, you are *gently* being forced to solve them. Don't wait until the *hammer drops*! Solve problems quickly.

The beginning of strife is as when one letteth out water: therefore leave off contention, before it be meddled with.

Proverbs 17:14

2626. What seemed like a dream will soon prove true. Through faith there's nothing that you and God can't do. Put your trust in God's Word. Put your hands to the plow. And what seemed like a dream will prove itself true now!

And the Lord answered me, and said, write the vision, and make it plain upon tables, that he may run that readeth it. For the vision is yet for an appointed time, but at the end it shall speak, and not lie: though it tarry, wait for it; because it will surely come, it will not tarry. Behold, his soul which is lifted up is not upright in him: but the just shall live by his faith.

Habakkuk 2:2-4

2627. God rewards action!

But without faith it is impossible to please him: for he that cometh to God must believe that he is, and that he is a rewarder of them that diligently seek him.

Hebrews 11:6

2628. Marriage is not an escape from life. Marriage is a *help* for life.

> And the Lord God said, it is not good that the man should be alone; I will make him an help meet for him.
>
> Genesis 2:18

2629. Regarding aging, you can't stop reality. You just have to plan for it.

> Hear counsel, and receive instruction, that thou mayest be wise in thy latter end.
>
> Proverbs 19:20

2630. Don't focus so much on waiting on your blessing to come toward you. Rather, focus on doing what's required so that you are moving toward your blessing. Then, and only then, is your blessing guaranteed!

> Even so faith, if it hath not works, is dead, being alone. Yea, a man may say, thou hast faith, and I have works: shew me thy faith without thy works, and I will shew thee my faith by my works.
>
> James 2:17-18

2631. Regarding endurance, life often requires you to go beyond the *yawn*.

In the morning sow thy seed, and in the evening withhold not thine hand: for thou knowest not whether shall prosper, either this or that, or whether they both shall be alike good.

> Ecclesiastes 11:6

2632. Regarding progress, every step in the right direction is a step worth taking.

The steps of a good man are ordered by the Lord: and he delighteth in his way.

> Psalm 37:23

2633. Because of the seeds of faith and obedience that you have already sown over your lifetime, God's blessings shall grow up and overtake your life like mighty green flourishing foliage in your future.

The righteous shall flourish like the palm tree: he shall grow like a cedar in Lebanon. Those that be planted in the house of the Lord shall flourish in the courts of our God. They shall still bring forth fruit in old age; they shall be fat and flourishing; To shew that the Lord is upright: he is my rock, and there is no unrighteousness in him.

> Psalm 92:12-15

2634. Regarding life, the source of frustration in real life is *unrealistic* demands.

There hath no temptation taken you but such as is common to man: but God is faithful, who will not suffer you to be tempted above that ye are able; but will with the temptation also make a way to escape, that ye may be able to bear it.

1 Corinthians 10:13

2635. Husbands, you are the head, but lead from your heart. Yet, use your head. A strong wife is an advantage. She is a gift of completion. She makes everything better. She causes you to be fruitful, multiply, replenish, subdue, and have dominion in the earth. You must be responsive to her influence and desires. Husbands, you are the head, but you must lead from your heart. Yet, use your head.

Wives, submit yourselves unto your own husbands, as unto the Lord. For the husband is the head of the wife, even as Christ is the head of the church: and he is the saviour of the body. Therefore as the church is subject unto Christ, so let the wives be to their own husbands in every thing. Husbands, love your wives, even as Christ also loved the church, and gave himself for it; That he might sanctify and cleanse it with the washing of water by the word, That he might present it to himself a glorious church, not having spot, or wrinkle, or any such thing; but that it should be holy and without blemish. So ought men to love their wives as their own bodies. He that loveth his wife loveth himself. For no man ever yet hated his own flesh; but nourisheth and cherisheth it, even as the Lord the church: For we are members of his body, of his flesh, and of his bones. For this cause shall a man leave his father and mother, and shall be joined unto his wife, and they two shall

be one flesh. This is a great mystery: but I speak concerning Christ and the church. Nevertheless let every one of you in particular so love his wife even as himself; and the wife see that she reverence her husband.

Ephesians 5:22-33

2636. Regarding caution, live like an old person, so that you can *become old*. I remember my Granddaddy saying, "I'm here by being careful." Therefore, regarding caution, live like an old person, so that you can *become old*.

Remember now thy Creator in the days of thy youth, while the evil days come not, nor the years draw nigh, when thou shalt say, I have no pleasure in them.

Ecclesiastes 12:1

2637. Regarding faith and reward, God is a gentleman. He made the first move, by making irrevocable promises, and initiating irreversible laws. We have to make the next move, by acting on what He promised. If we act in faith until completion, we will receive the exceedingly great and precious promises.

That by two immutable things, in which *it was* impossible for God to lie, we might have a strong consolation, who have fled for refuge to lay hold upon the hope set before us: which *hope* we have as an anchor of the soul, both sure and stedfast, and which entereth into that within the veil.

Hebrews 6:18-19

2638. You can't truly live your best life, until you die to your old life. There are things that must die in your life before you can live your best life *now*. Old things must pass away before all things can truly become new. Change starts with the extinguishing of old habits, hang-ups, and attitudes. Jesus is the source of true change. We must discipline ourselves to share in His crucifixion by the crucifying of our fleshy behavior. You can't truly live your best life until you die to your old life.

I am crucified with Christ: nevertheless I live; yet not I, but Christ liveth in me: and the life which I now live in the flesh I live by the faith of the son of God, who loved me, and gave himself for me.

Galatians 2:20

2639. Regarding beauty, roses are beautiful, but they can have thorns. However, a woman who fears the Lord, she shall be praised.

Favour is deceitful, and beauty is vain: but a woman that feareth the Lord, she shall be praised. Give her of the fruit of her hands; and let her own works praise her in the gates.

Proverbs 31:30-31

2640. Life is beautiful! Open yourself to God's possibilities in life! God will give you a colorful display of His splendor and blessings. Your best days are ahead! Life is beautiful! Wake up! Expect the best that life has to yield!

Now unto him that is able to do exceeding abundantly above all that we ask or think, according to the power that worketh in us.

Ephesians 3:20

2641. This is praying time. Prayer is not just an optional exercise. In the midst of today's unpredictable events in life, such as weather devastations, social atrocities, and potential military conflicts, prayer is crucial to survival. This is praying time. Prayer is not just an optional exercise.

If my people, which are called by my name, shall humble themselves, and pray, and seek my face, and turn from their wicked ways; then will I hear from heaven, and will forgive their sin, and will heal their land.

2 Chronicles 7:14

2642. If you eat dead food, you will die early. If you eat live food, you will live longer. Therefore, eat more live food.

Who satisfieth thy mouth with good things; so that thy youth is renewed like the eagle's.

Psalm 103:5

2643. When your heart is already inclined toward success, it doesn't take you long to make an obvious good decision; especially, when the benefits are obvious.

The thoughts of the diligent tend only to plenteousness; but of every one that is hasty only to want.

Proverbs 21:5

2644. Regarding your future, don't worry! God is committed to your future, and He's greater than your perception of your circumstances.

For I know the thoughts that I think toward you, saith the Lord, thoughts of peace, and not of evil, to give you an expected end.

Jeremiah 29:11

2645. It's better to *intentionally* make a decision, rather than to be *forced* to make a decision.

Multitudes, multitudes in the valley of decision: for the day of the Lord is near in the valley of decision.

Joel 3:14

2646. In a world prone to mistakes, don't be offended. Be prepared.

A prudent man foreseeth the evil, and hideth himself; but the simple pass on, and are punished.

Proverbs 27:12

2647. There's no triumph without a trial. There's no champion without a challenge.

Now thanks be unto God, which always causeth us to triumph in Christ, and maketh manifest the savour of his knowledge by us in every place.

2 Corinthians 2:14

2648. Ultimately, faith equals action of some kind. Even if that action is simply to stand and withstand the pressure that is fighting your faith.

Finally, my brethren, be strong in the Lord, and in the power of his might. Put on the whole armour of God, that ye may be able to stand against the wiles of the devil. For we wrestle not against flesh and blood, but against principalities, against powers, against the rulers of the darkness of this world, against spiritual wickedness in high places. Wherefore take unto you the whole armour of God, that ye may be able to withstand in the evil day, and having done all, to stand. Stand therefore, having your loins girt about with truth, and having on the breastplate of righteousness; And your feet shod with the preparation of the gospel of peace; Above all, taking the shield of faith, wherewith ye shall be able to quench all the fiery darts of the wicked. And take the helmet of salvation, and the sword of the spirit, which is the word of God: Praying always with all prayer and supplication in the spirit, and watching thereunto with all perseverance and supplication for all saints.

Ephesians 6:10-18

2649. Regarding doing business, there are some things that you learn from actually *doing* business that you can't learn any other way. However, *doing* does become easier when you have actually *studied* what to do.

And that ye study to be quiet, and to do your own business, and to work with your own hands, as we commanded you; that ye may walk honestly toward them that are without, and that ye may have lack of nothing.

1 Thessalonians 4:11-12

2650. Don't worry! Look up! God is still on the throne.

And he that sat was to look upon like a jasper and a sardine stone: and there was a rainbow round about the throne, in sight like unto an emerald.

Revelation 4:3

2651. It's dumb for those who don't know God to try to ridicule those who do know God. You could never be on the winning side when you are working against God.

And now I say unto you, refrain from these men, and let them alone: for if this counsel or this work be of men, it will come to naught: But if it be of God, ye cannot overthrow it; lest haply ye be found even to fight against God.

Acts 5:38-39

2652. God is a never ceasing flow of provision!

Now unto him that is able to do exceeding abundantly above all that we ask or think, according to the power that worketh in us.

Ephesians 3:20

2653. Spend time together with your family long enough so as to breathe the same air.

Can two walk together, except they be agreed?

Amos 3:3

2654. Excellence requires no explanation.

Where the word of a king is, there is power: and who may say unto him, what doest thou?

Ecclesiastes 8:4

2655. True wisdom challenges our current performance. Our current performance usually doesn't measure up to the proclaimed wisdom. However, the Lord sends the wisdom in order to give us the standard. Without the standard we wouldn't know what we should attempt to come up to.

And I will give you pastors according to mine heart, which shall feed you with knowledge and understanding. And it shall

come to pass, when ye be multiplied and increased in the land, in those days, saith the Lord, they shall say no more, the ark of the covenant of the Lord: neither shall it come to mind: neither shall they remember it; neither shall they visit it; neither shall that be done any more. At that time they shall call Jerusalem the throne of the Lord; and all the nations shall be gathered unto it, to the name of the Lord, to Jerusalem: neither shall they walk any more after the imagination of their evil heart.

Jeremiah 3:15-17

2656. The righteous don't run. The righteous are not intimidated. The righteous are not guilty. The righteous are not insecure. The righteous have no sense of inferiority. The righteous have no sense of condemnation. The righteous have no sense of inadequacy. The righteous *roar*! The righteous are bold as a *lion*!

The wicked flee when no man pursueth: but the righteous are bold as a lion.

Proverbs 28:1

2657. If you hold fast to your confession, then, you will hold fast to your faith.

That the communication of thy faith may become effectual by the acknowledging of every good thing which is in you in Christ Jesus.

Philemon 1:6

2658. All of the test and trials that you've been through have been to build your *faith muscles*. Trials build your faith muscles, because you're entering into a new place of blessing, but higher blessings require the use of some muscles that you may not have used previously. Higher places of blessing are not for *wimpy* people. It takes stronger faith muscles to be blessed. It takes stronger faith muscles to handle the responsibilities and challenges of the new place of blessing.

Then Isaac sowed in that land, and received in the same year an hundredfold: and the Lord blessed him. And the man waxed great, and went forward, and grew until he became very great: For he had possession of flocks, and possession of herds, and great store of servants: and the Philistines envied him.

Genesis 26:12-14

2659. May you behold the beauty that God continuously graces us with. May your life be painted with the brushstrokes of His amazing grace. May you always be enraptured by the splendor of His love. May your life express the expected blessings He's destined for your life! In Jesus name, amen.

I would seek unto God, and unto God would I commit my cause: Which doeth great things and unsearchable; marvellous things without number: Who giveth rain upon the earth, and sendeth waters upon the fields: To set up on high those that be low; that those which mourn may be exalted to safety.

Job 5:8-11

2660. Regarding communication in business, be willing to state the obvious in order to avoid giving place to misunderstanding.

Neither give place to the devil.

Ephesians 4:27

2661. In situations where the balance of power is not in your favor, or where attempting to win the *war of wills* may risk collateral damage, then, the only means by which to win is by the force of wisdom, compassion, patience, and better insight.

He that is slow to anger is better than the mighty; and he that ruleth his spirit than he that taketh a city.

Proverbs 16:32

2662. If you are a winner, then, you will win in life. What you already are will determine your true victory.

Now thanks be unto God, which always causeth us to triumph in Christ, and maketh manifest the savour of his knowledge by us in every place.

2 Corinthians 2:14

2663. Hold on! Don't give up now. Your best days are ahead. The best is yet to come. Don't forfeit your blessing and your children's blessing. Hold on. The best is yet to come!

The righteous also shall hold on his way, and he that hath clean hands shall be stronger and stronger.

Job 17:9

2664. Regarding contemporary life, there's right, there's wrong, and there's just plain *weird*! Some people live within the realm of right and wrong. Others cross the threshold into the realm of the weird, where the definitions are relative. However, God's eternal definition of right and wrong never changes. The rewards or consequences will determine whose definition is truly valid.

There are many devices in a man's heart; nevertheless the counsel of the Lord, that shall stand.

Proverbs 19:21

2665. I won't do certain things, because I know God is watching and I reverence God. I *do* certain things, because I respect God and I know that faith pleases God. It's all about the fear of God. The reverence of God should be the channel by which you determine everything that you do or don't do. Do you love God? Do you respect God? Then, that should determine what you do or don't do.

Let us hear the conclusion of the whole matter: fear God, and keep his commandments: for this is the whole duty of man. For God shall bring every work into judgment, with every secret thing, whether it be good, or whether it be evil.

Ecclesiastes 12:13-14

2666. Regarding questions, most questions are preceded by a preconceived conclusion.

The simple believeth every word: but the prudent man looketh well to his going.

Proverbs 14:15

2667. Life is a marathon. However, it's fulfilled by a series of determined *sprints*.

Know ye not that they which run in a race run all, but one receiveth the prize? So run, that ye may obtain. And every man that striveth for the mastery is temperate in all things. Now they do it to obtain a corruptible crown; but we an incorruptible. I therefore so run, not as uncertainly; so fight I, not as one that beateth the air: But I keep under my body, and bring it into subjection: lest that by any means, when I have preached to others, I myself should be a castaway.

1 Corinthians 9:24-27

2668. Regarding obeying God, it's not your job to know the future. It's your job to obey God *today*.

Now the Lord had said unto Abram, get thee out of thy country, and from thy kindred, and from thy father's house, unto a land that I will shew thee: And I will make of thee a great nation, and I will bless thee, and make thy name great; and thou shalt be a blessing: And I will bless them that bless thee, and curse him that curseth thee: and in thee shall all families of the earth be blessed. So Abram departed, as the Lord had spoken unto him; and lot went with him: and Abram was seventy and five years old when he departed out of Haran. And Abram took Sarai his wife, and lot his brother's son, and all their substance that they had gathered, and the souls that they had gotten in Haran; and they went forth to go into the land of Canaan; and into the land of Canaan they came.

Genesis 12:1-5

2669. Regarding you delivering your family from poverty, you have to dig yourself out of the ditch through diligence and determination. Then, you must continue to build a wall of protection and provision to keep the flood of poverty from ever encroaching again upon the shores of your family's inheritance.

A good man leaveth an inheritance to his children's children: and the wealth of the sinner is laid up for the just.

Proverbs 13:22

2670. Fruitfulness proves proper placement.

And God said, let us make man in our image, after our likeness: and let them have dominion over the fish of the sea, and over the fowl of the air, and over the cattle, and over all the earth, and over every creeping thing that creepeth upon the earth. So God created man in his own image, in the image of God created he him; male and female created he them. And God blessed them, and God said unto them, be fruitful, and multiply, and replenish the earth, and subdue it: and have dominion over the fish of the sea, and over the fowl of the air, and over every living thing that moveth upon the earth.

Genesis 1:26-28

2671. Regarding problems and productivity, your responsibility is just to "*Get 'er done!*" At the end of the day, excuses don't hold up. Therefore, just get it done.

In all labour there is profit: but the talk of the lips tendeth only to penury.

Proverbs 14:23

2672. The key to getting more out of life is to waste less time.

So teach us to number our days, that we may apply our hearts unto wisdom.

Psalm 90:12

2673. We may not have mastered every aspect of living according to the scripture. However, those who use God's Word as the framework for behavior for their lives will live a much more successful and peaceable life. Seek the Lord and obey His Word. It's the key to good living.

I beseech you therefore, brethren, by the mercies of God, that ye present your bodies a living sacrifice, holy, acceptable unto God, which is your reasonable service. And be not conformed to this world: but be ye transformed by the renewing of your mind, that ye may prove what is that good, and acceptable, and perfect, will of God. For I say, through the grace given unto me, to every man that is among you, not to think of himself more highly than he ought to think; but to think soberly, according as God hath dealt to every man the measure of faith. For as we have many members in one body, and all members have not the same office: So we, being many, are one body in Christ, and every one members one of another. Having then gifts differing according to the grace that is given to us, whether prophecy, let us prophesy according to the proportion of faith; Or ministry, let us wait on our ministering: or he that teacheth, on teaching; Or he that exhorteth, on exhortation: he that giveth, let him do it with simplicity; he that ruleth, with diligence; he that sheweth mercy, with cheerfulness. Let love be without dissimulation. Abhor that which is evil; cleave to that which is good. Be kindly affectioned one to another with brotherly love; in honour preferring one another; Not slothful in business; fervent in spirit; serving the Lord; Rejoicing in hope; patient in tribulation; continuing instant in prayer; Distributing to the necessity of saints; given to hospitality. Bless them which

persecute you: bless, and curse not. Rejoice with them that do rejoice, and weep with them that weep. Be of the same mind one toward another. Mind not high things, but condescend to men of low estate. Be not wise in your own conceits. Recompense to no man evil for evil. Provide things honest in the sight of all men. If it be possible, as much as lieth in you, live peaceably with all men. Dearly beloved, avenge not yourselves, but rather give place unto wrath: for it is written, vengeance is mine; I will repay, saith the Lord. Therefore if thine enemy hunger, feed him; if he thirst, give him drink: for in so doing thou shalt heap coals of fire on his head. Be not overcome of evil, but overcome evil with good.

Romans 12

2674. God's desire is for you to be rich, healthy, and happy!

Beloved, I wish above all things that thou mayest prosper and be in health, even as thy soul prospereth.

3 John 1:2

2675. I agree that there's a lot wrong with society. However, there's a lot of good stuff going on too. That's why we rejoice by choice and put our trust in the Lord for the rest. Do what we can to impact life. Continue in prayer. Trust God. He is still on the throne. He's faithful.

For our light affliction, which is but for a moment, worketh for us a far more exceeding and eternal weight of glory.

2 Corinthians 4:17

2676. When you don't need someone else's compliment to feel good about yourself, then, that's when you know you've really *got it going on*!

Do we begin again to commend ourselves? Or need we, as some others, epistles of commendation to you, or letters of commendation from you? Ye are our epistle written in our hearts, known and read of all men: Forasmuch as ye are manifestly declared to be the epistle of Christ ministered by us, written not with ink, but with the spirit of the living God; not in tables of stone, but in fleshy tables of the heart.

2 Corinthians 3:1-3

2677. To people who don't have an interesting life of their own, then, other people's life becomes very interesting to them. People who have an interesting and important life are too busy working on their own lives to be overly involved in anyone else's business.

And that ye study to be quiet, and to do your own business, and to work with your own hands, as we commanded you; that ye may walk honestly toward them that are without, and that ye may have lack of nothing.

1 Thessalonians 4:11-12

2678. Big people are too mature to become engrossed into childish games.

Brethren, be not children in understanding: howbeit in malice be ye children, but in understanding be men.

> 1 Corinthians 14:20

2679. Take time to build a *fence* against offense.

Seven times a day do I praise thee because of thy righteous judgments. Great peace have they which love thy law: and nothing shall offend them.

> Psalm 119:164-165

2680. It's normal to cease from growing externally. It's *optional* to cease from growing internally. Keep growing!

And he gave some, apostles; and some, prophets; and some, evangelists; and some, pastors and teachers; For the perfecting of the saints, for the work of the ministry, for the edifying of the body of Christ: Till we all come in the unity of the faith, and of the knowledge of the son of God, unto a perfect man, unto the measure of the stature of the fulness of Christ: That we henceforth be no more children, tossed to and fro, and carried about with every wind of doctrine, by the sleight of men, and cunning craftiness, whereby they lie in wait to deceive; But speaking the truth in love, may grow up into him in all things, which is the head, even Christ.

> Ephesians 4:11-15

2681. God, character, and investment into enriching knowledge and experiences determine the strength of the foundation of a marriage. God at the center of a marriage, the character of the two individuals, and the investments they make into the marriage will determine the strength of the foundation of a marriage.

There was in the days of Herod, the king of Judaea, a certain priest named Zacharias, of the course of Abia: and his wife was of the daughters of Aaron, and her name was Elisabeth. And they were both righteous before God, walking in all the commandments and ordinances of the Lord blameless.

Luke 1:5-6

2682. What did the complaining dog say about life? Life can be *ruff*!

All the days of the afflicted are evil: but he that is of a merry heart hath a continual feast.

Proverbs 15:15

2683. Just like the ground that you fertilize will become more fruitful, similarly, a life that you invest in will become more fruitful. A business that you invest in will become more fruitful. A marriage that you invest in will become more fruitful. Be a fertilizer of your life. Take time to read books, go to seminars, worship, pray, and read the Bible. Invest in the fruitfulness and productivity of your life and future.

He that tilleth his land shall be satisfied with bread: but he that followeth vain persons is void of understanding.

> Proverbs 12:11

2684. Help people, but obey God.

And whatsoever ye do, do it heartily, as to the Lord, and not unto men; knowing that of the Lord ye shall receive the reward of the inheritance: for ye serve the Lord Christ.

> Colossians 3:23-24

2685. Faith and love give you a good reputation with God. It causes you to receive more grace, favor, and power for living a successful life. Faith and love are the keys to successful living.

For in Jesus Christ neither circumcision availeth any thing, nor uncircumcision; but faith which worketh by love.

> Galatians 5:6

2686. Talk peace. Prepare for war.

If it be possible, as much as lieth in you, live peaceably with all men.

> Romans 12:18

2687. Sometimes to get to the next level, you have to negotiate with the devil.

Now the Philistines gathered together all their armies to Aphek: and the Israelites pitched by a fountain which is in Jezreel. And the Lords of the Philistines passed on by hundreds, and by thousands: but David and his men passed on in the rereward with Achish. Then said the princes of the Philistines, what do these Hebrews here? And Achish said unto the princes of the Philistines, is not this David, the servant of Saul the king of Israel, which hath been with me these days, or these years, and I have found no fault in him since he fell unto me unto this day? And the princes of the Philistines were wroth with him; and the princes of the Philistines said unto him, make this fellow return, that he may go again to his place which thou hast appointed him, and let him not go down with us to battle, lest in the battle he be an adversary to us: for wherewith should he reconcile himself unto his master? Should it not be with the heads of these men? Is not this David, of whom they sang one to another in dances, saying, Saul slew his thousands, and David his ten thousands? Then Achish called David, and said unto him, surely, as the Lord liveth, thou hast been upright, and thy going out and thy coming in with me in the host is good in my sight: for I have not found evil in thee since the day of thy coming unto me unto this day: nevertheless the Lords favour thee not. Wherefore now return, and go in peace, that thou displease not the Lords of the Philistines. And David said unto Achish, but what have I done? And what hast thou found in thy servant so long as I have been with thee unto this day, that I may not go fight against the enemies of my Lord the king?

And Achish answered and said to David, I know that thou art good in my sight, as an angel of God: notwithstanding the princes of the Philistines have said, he shall not go up with us to the battle. Wherefore now rise up early in the morning with thy master's servants that are come with thee: and as soon as ye be up early in the morning, and have light, depart. So David and his men rose up early to depart in the morning, to return into the land of the Philistines. And the Philistines went up to Jezreel.

1 Samuel 29

2688. We're living in a time where everything is *up for grabs*! Brand new powerhouses, brand new names, and brand new influencers are arriving on the world scene! This is a new day! This is a new opportunity for you to take your place in society. This is a time for you to take your place in history. There's nothing holding you back now! This is a new day! Everything's *up for grabs*! Everything is *up for grabs*! Take hold! Take hold of your success!

And from the days of John the Baptist until now the kingdom of heaven suffereth violence, and the violent take it by force.

Matthew 11:12

2689. You often hear some people talk about "A higher level brings a higher devil". However, the Bible says that "The blessing of the Lord makes rich, and he adds no sorrow with it." Often, the only reason a *"higher level"* of devil is released is, because, a *"great door"* is guarded by opposition. Yet, the

blessing is good. It's worth *fighting for*. Don't let fear keep you from possessing your blessing. God can give you a lifetime blessing of prosperity and peace. That's His promise!

The blessing of the Lord, it maketh rich, and he addeth no sorrow with it.

Proverbs 10:22

2690. You're halfway through the *halfway point* in the year. Now use all of your remaining strength to accomplish your main goals for the remainder of the year. Time moves fast. Focus is the key to fruitfulness.

So teach us to number our days, that we may apply our hearts unto wisdom.

Psalm 90:12

2691. Another day and another opportunity for a *million dollar idea*. Always keep an open mind, and a pen and paper near!

I wisdom dwell with prudence, and find out knowledge of witty inventions.

Proverbs 8:12

2692. "This little light of mine, I'm going to let it shine..." Your light shines so much more brilliantly in front of the backdrop of a darkening world. When the world gets darker,

the righteous will shine brighter, displaying God's beauty, grace, and wonder!

But the path of the just is as the shining light, that shineth more and more unto the perfect day.

Proverbs 4:18

2693. Let the righteous sing hallelujah! Let everyone that has breath praise the Lord! Praise ye the Lord!

Praise ye the Lord. Praise ye the Lord from the heavens: praise him in the heights. Praise ye him, all his angels: praise ye him, all his hosts. Praise ye him, sun and moon: praise him, all ye stars of light. Praise him, ye heavens of heavens, and ye waters that be above the heavens. Let them praise the name of the Lord: for he commanded, and they were created. He hath also stablished them for ever and ever: he hath made a decree which shall not pass. Praise the Lord from the earth, ye dragons, and all deeps: Fire, and hail; snow, and vapours; stormy wind fulfilling his word: Mountains, and all hills; fruitful trees, and all cedars: Beasts, and all cattle; creeping things, and flying fowl: Kings of the earth, and all people; princes, and all judges of the earth: Both young men, and maidens; old men, and children: Let them praise the name of the Lord: for his name alone is excellent; his glory is above the earth and heaven. He also exalteth the horn of his people, the praise of all his saints; even of the children of Israel, a people near unto him. Praise ye the Lord.

Psalm 148

2694. May the twins of *mercy and grace* shine upon you. May God's favor and compassion always be on display in your life, in Jesus name, amen!

Mercy and truth are met together; righteousness and peace have kissed each other. Truth shall spring out of the earth; and righteousness shall look down from heaven.

Psalm 85:10-11

2695. May the *"Sun of Righteousness"* arise upon your life with healing in His wings. May your joy be full and may your bank accounts be replete with increase!

But unto you that fear my name shall the sun of righteousness arise with healing in his wings; and ye shall go forth, and grow up as calves of the stall.

Malachi 4:2

2696. God's love is *spiritual*. It's not all in your head when you have it for another person. It's more than the *pathos* of feeling. It's more than the *eros* of the flesh. It's a commitment deeper than the soul. You just do the right thing for the other person, because you want to, even when you don't want to, because somehow the love of God has entered into your heart for the other person.

If ye fulfil the royal law according to the scripture, thou shalt love thy neighbour as thyself, ye do well.

James 2:8

2697. Regarding problems, don't put your head in the sand. Rather, develop a plan.

And they said, go to, let us build us a city and a tower, whose top may reach unto heaven; and let us make us a name, lest we be scattered abroad upon the face of the whole earth. And the Lord came down to see the city and the tower, which the children of men builded. And the Lord said, behold, the people is one, and they have all one language; and this they begin to do: and now nothing will be restrained from them, which they have imagined to do.

Genesis 11:4-6

2698. Regarding survival, people have been *making it* since we were made. God can take care of you.

Unto Adam also and to his wife did the Lord God make coats of skins, and clothed them.

Genesis 3:21

2699. Regarding solving problems, in most cases, it's not a matter of *rocket science*. In most cases, it's just a matter of *applying* the specific, reasonable knowledge that you already have.

To do justice and judgment is more acceptable to the Lord than sacrifice.

Proverbs 21:3

2700. If a person can't discern your rare, exquisite value, then, it's often futile to spend time explaining it to them. However, if you discern *their* value as being special to you, then, it is worth it to spend the necessary time explaining it to them, so that they can receive the value that you have been sent to give into their life.

When therefore the Lord knew how the Pharisees had heard that Jesus made and baptized more disciples than John, (though Jesus himself baptized not, but his disciples,) He left Judaea, and departed again into galilee. And he must needs go through Samaria. Then cometh he to a city of Samaria, which is called Sychar, near to the parcel of ground that Jacob gave to his son Joseph. Now Jacob's well was there. Jesus therefore, being wearied with his journey, sat thus on the well: and it was about the sixth hour. There cometh a woman of Samaria to draw water: Jesus saith unto her, give me to drink. (for his disciples were gone away unto the city to buy meat.) Then saith the woman of Samaria unto him, how is it that thou, being a Jew, askest drink of me, which am a woman of Samaria? For the Jews have no dealings with the Samaritans. Jesus answered and said unto her, if thou knewest the gift of God, and who it is that saith to thee, give me to drink; thou wouldest have asked of him, and he would have given thee living water. The woman saith unto him, sir, thou hast nothing to draw with, and the well is deep: from whence then hast thou that living water? Art thou greater than our father Jacob, which gave us the well, and drank thereof himself, and his children, and his cattle? Jesus answered and said unto her,

whosoever drinketh of this water shall thirst again: But whosoever drinketh of the water that I shall give him shall never thirst; but the water that I shall give him shall be in him a well of water springing up into everlasting life. The woman saith unto him, sir, give me this water, that I thirst not, neither come hither to draw. Jesus saith unto her, go, call thy husband, and come hither. The woman answered and said, I have no husband. Jesus said unto her, thou hast well said, I have no husband: For thou hast had five husbands; and he whom thou now hast is not thy husband: in that saidst thou truly. The woman saith unto him, sir, I perceive that thou art a prophet. Our fathers worshipped in this mountain; and ye say, that in Jerusalem is the place where men ought to worship. Jesus saith unto her, woman, believe me, the hour cometh, when ye shall neither in this mountain, nor yet at Jerusalem, worship the father. Ye worship ye know not what: we know what we worship: for salvation is of the Jews. But the hour cometh, and now is, when the true worshippers shall worship the father in spirit and in truth: for the father seeketh such to worship him. God is a spirit: and they that worship him must worship him in spirit and in truth. The woman saith unto him, I know that Messias cometh, which is called Christ: when he is come, he will tell us all things. Jesus saith unto her, I that speak unto thee am he. And upon this came his disciples, and marvelled that he talked with the woman: yet no man said, what seekest thou? Or, why talkest thou with her? The woman then left her water pot, and went her way into the city, and saith to the men, Come, see a man, which told me all things that ever I did: is not this the Christ?

John 4:1-29

2701. True success is successive.

Then Isaac sowed in that land, and received in the same year an hundredfold: and the Lord blessed him. And the man waxed great, and went forward, and grew until he became very great: For he had possession of flocks, and possession of herds, and great store of servants: and the Philistines envied him.

Genesis 26:12-14

2702. Regarding success, you don't need to invent the *wheel*. Rather, you need to *discover* the wheel. You may customize the wheels to fit your specific moneymaking vehicle. However, the *moneymaking wheels* of success are already turning.

Buy the truth, and sell it not; also wisdom, and instruction, and understanding.

Proverbs 23:23

2703. Never allow current circumstances to steal your expectation for the future.

But without faith it is impossible to please him: for he that cometh to God must believe that he is, and that he is a rewarder of them that diligently seek him.

Hebrews 11:6

Pastor Terrance Levise Turner, MBA

2704. Regarding your future, keep on praying and keep on living. The best is yet to come.

Build ye houses, and dwell in them; and plant gardens, and eat the fruit of them; Take ye wives, and beget sons and daughters; and take wives for your sons, and give your daughters to husbands, that they may bear sons and daughters; that ye may be increased there, and not diminished. And seek the peace of the city whither I have caused you to be carried away captives, and pray unto the Lord for it: for in the peace thereof shall ye have peace.

Jeremiah 29:5-7

2705. Creativity bypasses the realm of what's currently possible. Just because it hasn't been done, doesn't mean it can't be done. The idea just hasn't found a mind willing to receive it, believe it, and act upon it.

And Jesus went forth, and saw a great multitude, and was moved with compassion toward them, and he healed their sick. And when it was evening, his disciples came to him, saying, this is a desert place, and the time is now past; send the multitude away, that they may go into the villages, and buy themselves victuals. But Jesus said unto them, they need not depart; give ye them to eat. And they say unto him, we have here but five loaves, and two fishes. He said, bring them hither to me. And he commanded the multitude to sit down on the grass, and took the five loaves, and the two fishes, and looking up to heaven, he blessed, and brake, and gave the loaves to his disciples, and the disciples to the multitude. And

they did all eat, and were filled: and they took up of the fragments that remained twelve baskets full. And they that had eaten were about five thousand men, beside women and children.

Matthew 14:14-21

2706. You can't avoid life. You've just got to handle it.

There hath no temptation taken you but such as is common to man: but God is faithful, who will not suffer you to be tempted above that ye are able; but will with the temptation also make a way to escape, that ye may be able to bear it.

1 Corinthians 10:13

2707. God practices differentiation. Many businesses practice differentiation with their customers. They offer low-tier service. They offer basic service. They offer mid-level service. They offer executive level service. God will meet you according to your level of thinking and faith. As you increase in renewing your mind from that of the weak, desperate struggler, to that of a royal priest, king, ruler, and a god in the earth; then, you will see God deal with you in a different way. You will go from being dealt with as a servant, to being partnered with as a son or daughter and heir to the kingdom of God in the earth.

Now I say, that the heir, as long as he is a child, differeth nothing from a servant, though he be lord of all; But is under tutors and governors until the time appointed of the father.

Even so we, when we were children, were in bondage under the elements of the world: But when the fulness of the time was come, God sent forth his son, made of a woman, made under the law, To redeem them that were under the law, that we might receive the adoption of sons. And because ye are sons, God hath sent forth the spirit of his son into your hearts, crying, Abba, father. Wherefore thou art no more a servant, but a son; and if a son, then an heir of God through Christ.

Galatians 4:1-7

2708. Whether now or later, judgment day always comes.

Some men's sins are open beforehand, going before to judgment; and some men they follow after.

1 Timothy 5:24

2709. Sin is the root of all evil. Poverty is a branch of the cursed tree of sin and death. Satan planted the seed. The first man allowed Satan into his garden. Jesus came to uproot the seed of sin and deliver mankind from the curse of poverty, sin, sickness, disease, and death.

The spirit of the Lord is upon me, because he hath anointed me to preach the gospel to the poor; he hath sent me to heal the brokenhearted, to preach deliverance to the captives, and recovering of sight to the blind, to set at liberty them that are bruised, To preach the acceptable year of the Lord.

Luke 4:18-19

2710. There's nothing like the smile of an overcomer. Nothing tastes as good as *victory*!

Now thanks be unto God, which always causeth us to triumph in Christ, and maketh manifest the savour of his knowledge by us in every place.

2 Corinthians 2:14

Final Word

Now that you have enjoyed ***Distinguished Wisdom Presents... Living Proverbs–Vol. 5***, I encourage you to read this book daily. Use it as a reference book for continual counsel. Many readers of **"Living Proverbs"** series have indicated the words helped to deliver their mind. One reader even gave the book to a person addicted to drugs, and they were able to find wisdom for a better way of thinking. If the mind can get free, the life can get free. The words brought peace and deliverance. God's Word is a healer. As you renew your mind to His Word you will be set free. Proverbs 4:7 says, "Wisdom is the principal thing; therefore get wisdom: and with all thy getting get understanding." Therefore, I recommend that you take time to read this book over again, and allow these truths to free you. Jesus said these words in John 8:31–32 and 36:

> Then said Jesus to those Jews, which believed on him, If ye continue in my word, then are ye

my disciples indeed: And ye shall know the truth, and the truth shall make you free. If the son therefore shall make you free, you shall be free indeed.

God's Word is what makes us free. As we renew our mind to God's Word our lives will be changed. We will enjoy the best that He desires for us. And we will be able to teach our children, grandchildren, and those that we come in contact with how to be free indeed. Therefore, as you read this book **Distinguished Wisdom Presents... Living Proverbs–Vol.5**, my prayer is *"May your life be enriched by the words of wisdom!"* Be sure to look for the audiobook at www.TerranceTurnerLivingProverbs.com. Also, you can find other of my books at www.TerranceTurnerBooks.com. My books, as well as gospel music projects are also available on Amazon.com and your other favorites sites. Please look for these resources. You will be further enriched as you hear the words of the author in an audiobook, as well as experience anointed worship music from my wife and I, "Terrance & Avis Turner".

Pastor Terrance Levise Turner, MBA

About The Author

Pastor Terrance Levise Turner, MBA is the Senior Pastor of Faith Country Holiness Church, in Gallatin, TN. Pastor Turner has an MBA in Finance and Supply Chain Management from Tennessee State University. He also has a Bachelors degree in Speech Communications and Theater, with a concentration in Mass Media from Tennessee State University. He is president of Well Spoken Inc., a communications company, in Nashville, TN., which focuses on audiobooks, book publishing, and professional speaking. Pastor Turner is the author of several books, including the **Distinguished Wisdom Presents . . .*"Living Proverbs"* **series,** *Your Wealth Is In Your Anointing: Discover Keys To Releasing Your Potential*, and *The Dynamic Victory Confession: Powerful Confessions For A Victorious Life*. For more information visit www.TerranceTurnerBooks.com or www.TerranceTurnerLivingProverbs.com. Or email WellSpokenInc@bellsouth.net. Pastor Turner is also a songwriter and recording artist, with his wife, Dr. Avis Turner. His music is available on Amazon.com, ITunes, or at his website www.FaithCountryProductions.com. He continues to serve the community and Body of Christ through service, music, preaching and teaching the Word of God. He and his wife, Avis live in Nashville, TN.